Scribbling Women

&

The Real-Life Romance Heroes Who Love Them

Edited By
Hope Tarr

That Book, Inc., New York, New York

Copyright Acknowledgments

PART I: *How We Met*

"A Lost Friend, A Movie Star, A Friend to Love Forever"
© 2014 by Elf Ahearn

"Stuck on the Italian Boy"
© 2014 by Carole Bellacera

"Love at First Sight?"
© 2014 by Caryn Moya Block

"Socks with Sandals"
© 2014 by Katana Collins

"Donny and Me?"
© 2014 by Jacquie D'Alessandro

"A Leap of Faith Straight to the Altar"
© 2014 by Sonali Dev

"Falling in Love with the Intern"
© 2014 by Megan Frampton

"Acceptance"
© 2014 by Leanna Renee Hieber

"Unexpected Treasures"
© 2014 by Lisa Renée Jones

"Once Upon a Dream"
© 2014 by Delilah Marvelle

"Falling for My Husband"
© 2014 by Jen McLaughlin

"Once in a Blue Moon"
© 2014 by Deanna Raybourn

"Crossing the Pond"
© 2014 by Mary Rodgers

"Thanks to Uisce Beatha (Water of Life)"
© 2014 by Kat Simons

"Speeding Down the Relationship Super Highway"
© 2014 by Hope Tarr

Part II: *How We Wed*

"Wedding 101 for the Anti-Bridezilla"
© 2014 by Patience Bloom

"Holding Out for a Hero"
© 2014 by Leslie Carroll

"A 'Killer' Wedding"
© by J. Kenner

"Everything Is Perfect"
© 2014 by Elisabeth Staab

Part III: *How We Love*

"Real Life and Real Love"
© 2014 by Katharine Ashe

"Pasta for Dinner"
© 2014 by Suzan Cólon

"When You Come Home"
© 2014 by Carlene Love Flores

"Love Is All Around"
© 2014 by Donna Grant

"Resting Easy"
© 2014 by K.M. Jackson

"Soul Mates for a Thousand Lifetimes"
© 2014 by Jim and Nikoo McGoldrick

"For Better or For Worse"
© 2014 by Heather McCollum

"Working Our Way to a Happily Ever After"
© 2014 by Cindy Nord

"Catch Me When I Fall"
© 2014 by Sara Jane Stone

Scribbling Women & the Real-Life
Romance Heroes Who Love Them
© 2014 by Hope Tarr

Photo Credits

Elf Ahearn & Patrick with permission of the author
Katharine Ashe by Aimée Laine
Carole Bellacera & Frank with permission of the author
Caryn Moya Block & Mike courtesy of Booz Allen Hamilton
Patience Bloom & Sam by Chris Cozzone
Leslie Carroll & Scott by Matt Coleman
Katana Collins & Sean by BLAND Photography
Suzan Colón by Nathan Tweti
Jacquie D'Alessandro & Joe with permission of the author
Sonali Dev by Vernice Dollar of Studio 16
Carlene Love Flores with permission of the author
Megan Frampton & Scott by David Humphreys Photography
Donna Grant & Steve with permission of the author
Leanna Renee Hieber & Marcos with permission of the author
K.M. Jackson by Jax Cassidy
Lisa Renée Jones & Diego by Jennifer Jones, Luxe Photography, Austin, Texas
Julie Kenner with permission of the author
Delilah Marvelle & Marc with permission of the author
Jen McLaughlin & husband with permission of the author
Heather McCollum & Braden with permission of the author
Jim & Nikoo McGoldrick by Images of Watertown
Cindy Nord & Tom with permission of the author
Deanna Raybourn & husband with permission of the author
Mary Rodgers & Simon with permission of the author
Kat Simons by Biz Urban
Sara Jane Stone by Jenna Stern
Elisabeth Staab & Tom by Amy Czelusniak Studios
Hope Tarr & Raj with permission of the author

To the twenty-eight real-life romance heroes who inspired this book as well as those as yet unnamed and "unsung," gentlemen we salute you.

Contents

Acknowledgments ix
Foreword xi
A Note from Win xiii

PART I: *How We Met* 1

Donny and Me?
    By Jacquie D'Alessandro 3

Socks with Sandals
    By Katana Collins 9

Stuck on the Italian Boy
    By Carole Bellacera 18

Once Upon a Dream
    By Delilah Marvelle 23

A Leap of Faith Straight to the Altar
    By Sonali Dev 28

Falling for My Husband
    By Jen McLaughlin 34

Once in a Blue Moon
    By Deanna Raybourn 39

Love at First Sight?
    By Caryn Moya Block 44

Falling in Love with the Intern
    By Megan Frampton 48

Crossing the Pond
    By Mary B. Rodgers 52

Thanks to Uisce Beatha (Water of Life)
    By Kat Simons 57

Speeding Down the Relationship Super Highway
    By Hope Tarr 63

A Lost Friend, A Movie Star, A Man to Love Forever
    By Elf Ahearn 72

Contents

Acceptance
   By Leanna Renee Hieber   79
Unexpected Treasures
   By Lisa Renée Jones   85

PART II: *How We Wed*   91
A "Killer" Wedding
   By J. Kenner   93
Wedding 101 for the Anti-Bridezilla
   By Patience Bloom   98
Everything Is Perfect
   By Elisabeth Staab   106
Holding Out for a Hero
   By Leslie Carroll   111

PART III: *How We Love*   121
Pasta for Dinner
   By Suzan Colón   123
Catch Me When I Fall
   By Sara Jane Stone   128
Real Life & Real Love
   By Katharine Ashe   133
When You Come Home
   By Carlene Love Flores   139
Love Is All Around
   By Donna Grant   147
Working Our Way to a Happily Ever After
   By Cindy Nord   152
Resting Easy
   By K.M. Jackson   159
For Better or For Worse
   By Heather McCollum   165
Soul Mates for a Thousand Lifetimes; or, Diary of Two Cosmic Stalkers
   By Nikoo & Jim McGoldrick   172

Acknowledgments

My heartfelt thanks to the talented professionals who worked with me to turn what began as a kernel of an idea into an actual anthology. They are, in no particular order:

Lori Perkins, owner of the L. Perkins Agency as well as co-founder of Riverdale Avenue Books, for generously sharing her publishing knowledge.

My ever-wonderful agent, Louise Fury of The Bent Agency, for her generous support and invaluable advice.

Emily Keyes for availing me of her contract expertise when I needed it most.

The very talented Joyce Lamb, freelance copy editor and founder/curator of *USA Today's* Happy Ever After romance novels blog, for her stellar copy-editing services.

My talented cover artist, Rachel Marks, and book formatter, 52 Novels, for helping to transform a "mysterious" process into one that felt imminently doable.

Lastly, to my amazing contributing authors, all of whom agreed—without hesitation—to waive *any* monetary compensation on behalf of raising funds for the charity and who took time away from their deadlines, families, and other commitments to share their wonderful real-life love stories. You ladies (and gentleman) are what make the romance fiction community one to which I will always be proud to belong.

Foreword

"America is now wholly given over to a damned mob of scribbling women, and I should have no chance of success while the public taste is occupied with their trash—and should be ashamed of myself if I did succeed."
—Nathaniel Hawthorne,
1855 letter to his publisher,
William D. Ticknor

More than 150 years later, Hawthorne's words still snap with the same bitter bite. How is it that the author of *The Scarlet Letter* could evoke such rancor for his sisters of the quill? Fortunately, for every Hawthorne there is a real-life romance hero who stands by his or her "scribbling woman" without failure or faltering, with enduring support and dragon-slaying devotion. Regardless of whether our book reviews are good or bad, whether we make a bestseller list or continue to strive toward that goal, whether dinner is Julia Child divine or, more likely, takeout pizza *again*, he is always there, covering our backs and sometimes flanking our computer chairs, bearing silent or not-so-silent witness to his support, his belief in us—and, above all, his love.

And so the idea for this nonfiction anthology was born. In it, twenty-eight popular romance novelists, one for each day of February 2014, share the real-life stories of how they met, wed and love their spouse or romantic partner. Some journeys to True Love involved travel, even relocation, to or from overseas

Foreword

(Ireland, England, India); others took place in writers' own backyards. Some couples met as college sweethearts, others as seasoned second-chance lovers. Some of the essays are tongue in cheek, even laugh-out-loud funny, while others are poignant, even bittersweet. All affirm that Happily Ever After isn't only the stuff of fairy tales and romance novels.

It is every woman's *birthright*.

Because we believe that, passionately and purposefully, all net proceeds from sales of *Scribbling Women and the Real-Life Romance Heroes Who Love Them* will support Win, formerly known as Women in Need. (All authors contributed their essays for free.) Since its February 14, 1983, founding, Win has worked tirelessly to bring the hope of Happily Ever After to disadvantaged women and their children in New York City, empowering them to build positive, independent lives and forge forward into brighter futures. (A note from Win President and CEO Bonnie Stone follows.)

Wishing you a Valentine's month filled with fairy-tale dreams come true,

Hope Tarr
February 2014, New York, NY

A Note from Win

Thirty years ago, Win opened its doors on Valentine's Day. It wasn't planned to coincide with a holiday about love, but that's how it was born. Until this time, there were no services for homeless families with children. Win was founded to help those most in need, and on that day in February, the first Win families—four women and their children—were provided with emergency, temporary shelter in the basement of the Church of Saint Mary the Virgin in Midtown Manhattan.

Arriving at Win during the most tumultuous time in their lives, these families were met with support, guidance and care, and their children were provided with structure, sometimes for the first time. As the need to help these homeless families grew, so did Win. Over the next few years, Win opened more shelters in Manhattan, Brooklyn and the Bronx, providing families with safe, clean shelter and access to critical services, including child care, substance-abuse counseling, domestic-violence services, money management, employment readiness and life skills. Understanding that homelessness is a result of many different issues, Win treats each family uniquely, so that the issues they face are personally addressed.

For more than thirty years, Win has transformed the lives of New York City homeless women and their children by providing a holistic solution of safe housing, critical services and groundbreaking programs they need to succeed on their own—so the

A Note from Win

women can regain their independence and their children can look forward to a brighter future. Everyone deserves a happily ever after, especially Win's families.

Bonnie Stone
President and CEO
Win
115 West 31st Street, 7th floor
New York, NY 10001
winnyc.org

PART I

How We Met

Donny and Me?

Jacquie D'Alessandro

The first boy I ever loved was Donny Osmond. A poster of him graced my bedroom wall, and thanks to *Tiger Beat* magazine (which sucked up all my allowance), I knew all things Donny—his birthday (December 9), favorite color (purple), as well as the words to every song on every album he recorded. The Osmond brothers were the first concert I ever attended (at Madison Square Garden; I was in the fourth grade), and Donny was the recipient of the one and only fan letter I've ever written. To prove the depth of my devotion: I was the only kid in the neighborhood who didn't go to summer recreation because it started at 8 A.M., and even as a child I wasn't an early riser. Yet, when the Osmonds starred in a Saturday morning cartoon that aired at 8 A.M., I was not only awake, I was dressed and had my hair combed and teeth brushed ('cause I had to look nice for Donny, you know!) and was glued to the television. And even though I lived in New York and he lived in Utah, my ten-year-old lovesick self was convinced we'd someday meet and fall in love.

Yeah, that totally didn't happen.

What did happen was a public speaking class in college. The first assignment was to teach the class about something. I sat in the front row and watched a student walk to the front of the room.

My first thought was, "Wow, he looks like Donny Osmond!"

Now, you'd think this would have been my first clue that this was Mr. Right—right? Yes, I guess it should have been, but it wasn't. In my defense, I can only say that at that point I was only nineteen and I wasn't looking for Mr. Right. I wanted my freedom and independence to travel and learn who the heck I was.

Anyway, the Donny look-alike's name was Joe, and for the assignment he was going to teach the class how to play poker. He stood in front of me, looking all cute and Donny-like, then cut the deck of cards he held with one hand.

My second thought was, "Hmmm. Good hands." (Yes, yes, I know that should have been clue number two that this was My Future, but again, I wasn't long-term planning at that point.)

Yet, while I wasn't looking for a serious boyfriend, I was more than happy to be friends with the adorable Joe. We soon became good buds, walking to classes together and going to the on-campus game room, where he proved those hands really were good by trouncing me at Space Invaders (very popular in 1980). In addition to being cute, he was smart (like help-me-with-my-incomprehensible-computer-science-homework-so-I-could-pass-the-class smart) and funny. It worked out great that I wasn't looking for a serious boyfriend, because he had zero time for a serious girlfriend. In addition to being a full-time student, Joe was holding down three part-time jobs to pay for his tuition, books, and car expenses. Between that and my classes and my own part-time job, we didn't actually go on a date until two months after we'd met.

We didn't have anything out of the ordinary planned for that first date—just a movie on campus (*The Seduction of Joe Tynan* starring Alan Alda). When Joe picked me up at my parents' house (like many Hofstra students, Joe and I both lived at home and commuted daily to school), I was upstairs in my bedroom getting ready. I heard him talking to my parents downstairs, then a few minutes later I heard someone playing the piano. I knew immediately it had to be Joe. He'd mentioned he played, but I'd never heard him. After a few notes, I recognized the song: Frankie Valli's "Can't Take My Eyes Off You." When I came downstairs, he said he'd learned the song for me.

Now, even though we were just friends and this was a casual date, I have to admit, I was impressed.

Yup, and so were my parents. My dad, a piano player as well, was soon talking chord progressions with Joe. My mom pulled me aside and whispered, "We like this one!"

I liked him, too, and over the course of the semester and into the next one, Joe and I continued to casually date, going out about once a month as our busy schedules allowed. We got along great, had a lot in common, enjoyed the same things (yes, I know—a bazillion He's Mr. Right clues!). But in spite of all that, I still wasn't interested in having a serious boyfriend. I wanted to learn about me—who I was, what was important to me, and what didn't matter all that much. I wanted to be independent, to travel, to see the world. And even if I had wanted a serious boyfriend, Joe had no time for a serious girlfriend.

Or so I thought. After about a year of this casual dating, Joe told me he wanted more. Unfortunately, at the ripe old age of twenty, I still didn't feel ready to commit. He was hurt, which made me feel bad (really, really bad), but I knew it would be a mistake to try to give him something I wasn't ready to give. We didn't have any more classes together and went our separate ways. I figured that in spite of all those clues to the contrary, that was it for us.

But then, shortly before we graduated, we met on campus by chance and briefly caught up with each other. I told him I'd gotten a management job with TWA, and he'd scored a job with one of the Big Eight accounting firms in Manhattan. We parted on friendly terms, wished each other well, but a few weeks later, we both graduated and completely lost touch.

Fast-forward a year: Out of the blue I received a call from Joe. He recalled I worked for TWA, and he was planning a month-long trip to Europe and wondered if I could provide him with any travel info. I agreed, and we met at a Red Lobster for lunch. I gave him a bunch of travel brochures, told him about some of the places I'd visited and loved (London, Madrid, Rome), then we talked about his travel plans, which were very open—he wanted to train his way to as many cities as he could visit in a month's time. When lunch ended, he thanked me for all the info, then asked if we could get together when he returned from his trip. It was clear that he had a date in mind, so I told him I was dating someone and it was pretty serious, so while a date couldn't happen, I'd love to hear how the trip went.

Joe sent me a postcard from Europe, and he called me when he returned. He told me all about his fabulous trip, and when he finished, he asked me out to dinner. And that's when I told him that while he was away I'd gotten engaged to the guy I'd been seriously dating. He congratulated me, wished me all the best, and that was it.

Well, not exactly. The problem was that I was only engaged for a few weeks when I realized I was making a mistake. The man I'd become engaged to was a good person, and I cared for him deeply, but I knew in my heart he wasn't The One. He hadn't done anything wrong, but he just wasn't the *right* person. I waited a few more weeks before breaking things off with him, just to be certain I was doing the right thing and truly knew my own mind. But I was sure. I wasn't engaged to the right man.

Now, at that point, I wasn't positive Joe was necessarily Mr. Right—I only knew the man I was engaged to wasn't him. After I gave back the ring and ended my engagement, I took a bit of time to reassess and get myself back together again.

And then I called Joe.

I'll never forget that phone call. Keeping in mind that this was the days before cell phones, his sister answered. She told me Joe was in Indianapolis for the week for work and staying at the Marriott. I called the hotel and was connected to Joe's room. When he answered, it was clear there was a party going on—lots of laughing and noise and chatter. Joe explained that since he'd been at the hotel for several weeks for work, he was a "regular," and at his request a small piano had been moved into his suite. All his co-workers were there, and Joe was playing Beatles songs. I told him I was calling to tell him I wasn't engaged any longer, and I wanted to know if his dinner invite was still open. He didn't say yes—he shouted it. I wasn't sure if that was because he was really happy or just because it was so noisy, but I took it as a good sign. He told me, months later, that when I told him I was engaged, he'd actually cried—a sentiment I thought was so sweet it made *me* cry.

That phone call took place in September 1984, and by the following spring I was sure Joe was The One and I knew he felt the same. In July 1985, we went to a Chinese restaurant for dinner after work. Joe was acting really weird—very nervous, which was odd, as he's normally very calm. After dinner I excused myself to visit the ladies' room. Now, this might fall under the category of Too Much Information, but it's pertinent to the story, so here it is. Back in 1985, women wore pantyhose. It was July and it was hot, and after using the facilities, I had a heck of a time pulling those stupid pantyhose up my sweaty legs. It was like trying to put toothpaste back in the tube. Because it was a difficult feat—one I was determined to accomplish without destroying my hose—I was gone for a bit of time. When I returned to the table, Joe had this unnerved look on his face. He said, "What took you so long? Dessert is here!" He pointed to a silver bowl with a scoop of half-melted chocolate ice cream with a fortune cookie on top.

Since I didn't really want to explain the sweaty legs/pantyhose problem, I just said, "Sorry," but I was thinking, *Wow, he must have had a really bad day at the office.*

I picked up my somewhat soggy fortune cookie, broke it open, and pulled out the fortune. It read: *I love you very much.* I turned it over. The other side read: *Will you marry me?*

At least now I understood why he'd been acting as if he had a grenade in his pants all evening. I looked him in the eyes (his were wide and very deer-in-the-headlights), leaned across the table and whispered, "Honey, I think the waiter *really* likes me."

For several seconds, he didn't say anything. Then all the color drained from his face. "The waiter didn't write that," he said, sounding totally panicked. "*I* did!"

I instantly felt bad for teasing him, because there was no doubt he was totally freaked out. I assured him I knew he'd written it and told him yes. Yes, yes, yes! The next day he sent me a dozen roses, and we began a yearlong engagement that culminated in a beautiful wedding. Four and a half years later we welcomed our son, Christopher, who has grown into an amazing young man. He graduated college last year and now runs an organic farm. Last year, for our twenty-seventh anniversary, Joe and I visited Las Vegas.

He bought me front-row tickets to the Donny and Marie show—so I could see the first boy I ever loved with the last boy I'll ever love.

And that is just one of the gazillion reasons why I still love him all these years later and why he is at the heart of every hero I've ever written.

New York Times and *USA Today* bestselling author Jacquie D'Alessandro has written more than thirty books spanning the historical, paranormal, contemporary romantic comedy, women's fiction, and non-fiction genres. Her books have been published in over twenty-one languages. Jacquie grew up on Long Island, New York, graduated from Hofstra University and now lives in Georgia with her husband and son. No matter what genre she's writing in, all of Jacquie's books are filled with two of her favorite things—love and laughter.

Visit her online at www.jacquied.com.

Socks with Sandals

KATANA COLLINS

It was painfully humid out and beads of sweat gathered at the nape of my neck as we walked the five blocks to the art supply store. I was a freshman in college and had just met Eliza, the girl who would become my lifelong best friend.

The store was swarming with students. The air conditioner hummed from above and goose bumps covered my glistening arms as it spit frigid air over my body in short, sharp hisses. My corduroy overalls made a *zip* noise as the pant legs brushed against each other and the straps kept falling off my shoulders, down past my dark blue shirt. The stiff material brushed against the soft skin of my bicep. I could feel the handkerchief I wore as a headband starting to slip, and I tugged it back into place between pinched fingers.

I reached for something called a rubber brayer. As my fingertips brushed the hard plastic casing, a deep voice spoke quietly from my right side. "You won't use that. They always say to buy it, but I've been drawing for years and have never needed one."

I looked to the right without moving my head, my body frozen in its position. He was tall, towering more than a foot over me. He had chiseled features: an angular nose, a strong chin and a jawline so sharp, it could slice through glass. His brow bone was so pronounced that it cast a shadow over deep-set blue eyes. His muscles rippled beneath his black wifebeater, and he wore faded jeans and Chucks. Two earrings hung from the cartilage of his left ear, and his light brown hair, though short, curled around the outside of the bandanna he had tied around his head.

I released the tool that was in my hand. All I could answer was, "Oh."

He nodded and brushed past me, not smiling but not frowning. Not much of a talker, apparently.

After about thirty minutes, my basket was full of pencils, charcoal, paint, brushes, newsprint, and any other generic art supply you could think of. Eliza and I were already heading to the long checkout line, and when we reached the end, we prepared ourselves for a long wait. Standing directly in front of me was the guy in the orange bandanna. Eliza didn't seem to notice him. I quickly turned my back to him. Still, I kept shifting my weight back and forth, knowing he was within earshot.

Eliza's basket was spilling with even more junk than mine, and she rummaged through it, making sure she hadn't missed anything from her list. "Are you taking any photography classes this quarter?"

"No. I probably could have switched my schedule in order to, but I figured that's what everyone would be trying to do." The metal handle of my basket was starting to pinch the skin on my forearm, so I shifted it to the other side.

Eliza still didn't look up. "Yeah, I saw my advisor today. I didn't want to have to wait to start classes within my major."

There was a huff, a stifled laugh, from bandanna guy in front of us. Eliza looked confused, and my eyebrows rose defensively. I continued, ignoring his outburst. "Did you manage to get a theater class in, too?"

Eliza was still looking over my shoulder at the guy behind me. "No, I could only choose one battle, so I went with photography." After she finished this sentence, she mouthed the words, *Do you know him?*

I shook my head, and when I turned to look over my shoulder, he was already glancing in my direction with an arrogant tip to his lips. "That's true," I looked back at Eliza. "I figured since I was auditioning for the fall musical, I didn't need to take a theater class right now."

This time he belly-laughed, without even attempting to swallow or hide it.

"Excuse me." I spun to face him. "Does our conversation amuse you?"

He put a closed fist in front of his mouth, trying to compose himself. "I'm sorry." He said the words, but they just didn't seem sincere. "It just explains so much." He said this in a way that suggested I was supposed to know what he was talking about. He paused, and I raised my eyebrows, my gaze returning his blankly. He continued, "You know. *You.* Being an actress." His smile was bright and showed a row of beautifully straight teeth.

My eyes narrowed. "Yes, I am an actress. And that explains what exactly? My natural charm? My ability to clearly catch your attention?"

"I was gonna say your loud mouth." He laughed, mischief flashing in his crystal-blue eyes. "So what are you doing at this school? Acting is hardly an art form."

He was trying to get a rise out of me. I felt like I was back in kindergarten, and he was the boy who sat behind me, tugging on my braids. "You've obviously never seen *me* act, then."

"Touché."

"So what is it *you* study, Mr. Arteest."

He cleared his throat. "Well, I am a sequential art major." He stopped there, without further explanation.

"And what is that exactly?" I tried to elongate my spine to appear taller in front of him.

"It's, uh, like illustration."

Eliza cut in, her voice sharp. "Sequential art isn't illustration...it's comic book art."

I laughed louder than I intended and had to press my lips together in order to stop. "Let me get this straight...in your mind, comics are more of an art form than theater?"

His long arm reached around, rubbing the back of his neck. "To be fair, *I* never claimed to be an artist, either." He grinned. "Which dorm did they put you in?"

"Turner," I answered, nodding my head in the direction.

"How's the food there? Pretty bad?"

"No, actually," I said. "It surprised me how good it was."

With a quirk of his lips, he opened his mouth to say more as the sales associate at the register shouted, "Next!" I could have thrown my charcoal right at her face for interrupting us. Bandanna guy made his way to the counter, taking a moment to glance once more at me from over his shoulder.

I paid first, leaving Eliza inside at a register and went outside for a reprieve from the frigid air conditioner. As I pushed open the doors, I saw him waiting there for me, leaning against the brick of the building with one foot propped up behind him. I smiled and shielded my eyes from the bright sunlight. "Well, hey again."

"Hi." He was squinting one eye tighter than the other in the sunlight. "So I was thinking, the dorm food *can't* be that good." He spoke in an exaggerated tone. "You need a real meal. Like at a restaurant. With me."

I smiled, dropping my one free hand down to my thigh. "I think you're right."

"I'm Sean." He handed me a piece of paper with his name and number on it. As his hand reached across to mine, I noticed him looking intently at my bag. His direction shifted, and he reached in and pulled out the rubber brayer from before. "I thought I told you that you didn't need this."

I plucked it from his grasp and tossed it back into my bag. "I don't trust a man's opinion who doesn't consider what I do an art form." While I was saying this, Eliza came outside carrying two shopping bags.

I brushed past his shoulder, and as we were walking Eliza leaned in to me. "You really *don't* need that, you know."

I didn't look at her but spoke through the side of my mouth. "Shh, I know. I'm returning it tomorrow."

He was picking me up at 7:30 P.M. I had an hour to get ready, although it had been all I thought about all day. Eliza sat on my bed as I rummaged through my closet, desperate to find the perfect outfit.

My head was tucked between clothing that draped off of hangers. Spotting a colorful blue and brown wrap dress, I seized it with my right hand, flinging it off of its hanger and held it up to my body. "Yes?"

Scrunching her nose, Eliza shook her head. "It's trying too hard." She had a point. And what if he showed up in jogging shorts and Adidas running shoes? I didn't know where he was taking me. I had to go with something casual that also looked mature, especially since the first and only time we had met, I was wearing overalls. I bit my lip and fell onto my bed into a heap of clothes I had already looked through. The clock on my nightstand blinked *6:38*. Less than an hour to pick an outfit, style my hair, and do my makeup. I originally thought this would be plenty of time. It had never taken me more than half an hour to prepare for a date in high school. But, then again, I had never been asked out by someone as old as Sean before. He was almost twenty-one. I had just turned eighteen a month before. He was a junior. I was a freshman. As an eighteen-year-old girl, this age difference felt wild and dangerous. And it baffled me; I hardly seemed his type. He was tall, muscular, worked out constantly, was on crew. And I was…well, I was me. A typical teenage girl fresh off the bus from the suburbs. Wide-eyed, driven to change the world, and not yet tainted by its sadistic jokes. I sat up, leaning on my elbows. On the floor lay my crumpled jeans I had worn to class that day. They were a dark stonewash color and still clean. Well, basically clean. I sprang off my elbows, grabbing them and a few other articles and scuttled into my bathroom to change. I emerged from the bathroom wearing the jeans, which sat low on my hips in an understated, sexy way, a long-sleeved dark green boatneck shirt, a snakeskin belt with a sparkly marcasite buckle, and faux snakeskin mules that peeked out from under the hems of my jeans. Liza's eyes lit as she saw me, a smile spreading wide across her face, and she clapped as if I had just given an amazing performance.

I was wearing my brown plastic-rimmed glasses and Liza sprang off the bed. Walking at me, she reached out and yanked the glasses off my face. "Overkill."

"Liza, those weren't just for show. I can't *see* without them."

Fifty-two minutes later, I had put my contacts in, straightened my hair, and put on makeup—even eyeliner, which I absolutely detested. No matter how I tried, I always ended up poking myself in the eyeball.

"Well?" I held out my hands, doing a little twirl.

Eliza nodded, approving. "Perfect."

There was a knock at my door; two large thumps that caused me to jump nervously. I forced myself to walk slowly to the door, my legs itching to run, and when I looked behind me, Eliza had jumped up as well and was following at my heels. "Be cool," I whispered at her, which she answered with an exaggerated eye roll.

I swung the door open, and there he stood. He was as good-looking as I remembered him being. Wearing aviator sunglasses despite it being twilight, a red plaid shirt with the buttons open, revealing a gray wifebeater underneath, dark jeans, and lastly, when I reached his feet…open sandals with bright white socks. I inwardly groaned, hoping Eliza wouldn't notice the last detail.

He removed his sunglasses, and his eyes traveled the length of my body, leaving a shiver on my spine in its wake. If he was trying to be subtle, he failed miserably. "Wow, you look great," he said.

"Thanks," I sighed, relieved that I hadn't worn a dress. "You don't look so bad yourself." I smiled back at him. He leaned to the right, looking over my shoulder. "Hey, Liza. Good to see you again."

"Should we get going?"

"Sure." He smiled. "Oh, you should grab a jacket. It's supposed to get chilly tonight." I turned to go into my closet but realized if I were to do so, he would see what a mess it was. In my frenzy of getting ready, I hadn't thought to clean up a little. I made a mental note for next time.

Sensing the panic in my eyes, Eliza handed me her denim jacket that was draped over her arm. "Here," she said, "I forgot you wanted to borrow this tonight." I exhaled my held breath and reached out to take it from her, silently mouthing, *Thank you*. She sent me a wink as the jacket slipped from her grip.

Our dinner was lovely and casual. Conversation flowed as easily as the chocolate fudge out of the lava cake we shared. The restaurant was only a short drive from the beach, and after dinner, we found ourselves walking along the pier.

His hand snaked into mine, lacing our fingers. His eyes widened. "Your hands are freezing."

Even with Liza's jacket, I was still cold, the wind from the ocean whipping around our faces, whistling a romantic tune in our ears. It was crazy to me how drastically the weather could change down here along the ocean. His hands curled around my waist and lifted me onto the railing of the pier. Taking off his fleece, he pulled it over my head.

A moment passed as his gaze lingered on my face. As though he was taking inventory of every little detail. I fidgeted and rubbed my hands together to rid myself of the chill. I slipped off my shoes and carried them in one hand when we resumed walking.

The sand was refreshing and cool as it squished between my toes. Without my realizing it, he had stopped walking, giving my hand a tug and swinging me around so that we were face-to-face. My breath shortened and caught in the back of my throat. Tilting my chin with his index finger, he lowered his face to mine and kissed me. The warmth of his mouth branded my lips, and I stiffened against him. It was a man's kiss. A man's desire. The first kiss I'd ever experienced that truly made me feel like a woman. A tornado rushed from where his lips touched mine and spiraled all the way down my body to my toes. I was immediately warm again, pleasure ripping through my senses. He ended the kiss, his blue eyes darkening. Instead of going in for a second kiss, he wrapped his arms tighter around me and picked me up in an embrace. My nose buried into the curve of where his neck turned into his shoulder, and my lips eventually rested there. His skin tasted salty like the ocean. He lowered me back to the sand, and my arms unraveled from his neck, squeezing the taut muscles at his shoulders. I was dizzy and feared I would fall if I let go too quickly. His skin, though tan, looked nearly translucent in the moonlight. He pressed his forehead to mine and reached up to cover one of my hands with his. Lowering it to his side, we continued walking, but in the opposite direction, back to his car. Ocean waves crashed against the jetties and then fizzled, retreating deeper into the sea.

There was something about this guy. He was funny, sexy, a body so chiseled you would think it to be carved from marble. But still, as we walked along, something turned over in my stomach. Compared to him, I was just barely an adult. He was like a Gucci suit. Everything about it was perfect. Expertly crafted and tailored to fit just right. On paper, there were absolutely no flaws. But when you went to try it on your body, something was off. Perhaps the seam was at a weird angle. Maybe it just wasn't cut for your body. Or maybe you just needed to grow into it a little more.

If I could just grow a little more, Sean might be the perfect suit for me. That is, if I could break his habit of wearing socks with sandals.

For as long as she can remember Katana Collins always had one of two things in hand—a pen or a camera. And now, after thirty years, she is lucky enough to have two of the best jobs ever—writing sexy romances and photographing sexy boudoir portraits. Katana's debut novel, *Soul Stripper*, released in June 2013, followed soon after by its sequel, *Soul Survivor*, in September 2013. When not writing, reading, or photographing, you can find Katana with her husband and two dogs in Brooklyn, where she drinks copious amounts of coffee and red wine and actively volunteers her time and photography expertise to local animal shelters.

Visit her online at www.katanacollins.com
or follow her on Twitter @katanacollins.

Stuck on the Italian Boy

CAROLE BELLACERA

Frank swears he remembers the first time we met. I don't think he does. It's been thirty-nine years since that fateful morning in Crete when I first laid eyes on my future husband, the handsome Italian boy from the Bronx. I saw him as soon as he walked into the Iraklion Air Station clinic where I worked as a medical technician in the Air Force. He was just my type—tall and slender with curly black hair, a strong Roman nose, a sexy black moustache (all the rage in those days) and gorgeous soft-brown eyes. Even in his 1505s tan uniform with his name scrawled across a navy blue strip, he looked like a double for folk singer Jim Croce.

Bell-ack-er-a. I sounded it out in my head. *What a weird name.* But he sure was cute.

I knew why he was here. He'd come in for a flu shot—and lucky me, I was the one administering it. Sensing he was nervous, I gave him a reassuring smile. Typical guy. Trying to act like an injection was no big deal, but I could see just a glimmer of anxiety in those velvety brown eyes.

"Don't worry," I said, rubbing a cotton ball soaked with alcohol over his olive-skinned bicep. "You might feel a little pinch."

He barely grimaced when the needle went in, and just like that, it was over. I placed a Band-Aid over the tiny puncture hole and gave his arm a pat. "Good as new. It might feel a little achy for a while."

He gave me a sweet smile and spoke with a thick New York accent. "The best shot I ever had. Thanks, Red."

I watched him go, wondering if I'd ever see him again.

To this day, I really don't believe Frank remembers me giving him that shot. He denies it, of course, joking that he's been "stuck on me" ever since, but I think that's only because I told him we'd met before.

The story *he* remembers—and the one that will live on as an eternal joke with our friends and family—is the story of how we met *the second time*.

Fast-forward a couple of weeks from the flu shot meeting. On a warm spring night in April, I left my dorm with a girlfriend and decided to check out an impromptu party in progress between the two dorms. Boyfriendless at the time, I kind of automatically swept the crowd in search of a "potential"—and stopped on Frank.

I recognized him immediately. Feeling unusually brave, I parked myself next to him and immediately engaged him in conversation. Oh, how I loved his sexy New York accent. Terribly exotic for a girl who'd grown up in the cornfields of Indiana. But it wasn't just his good looks and accent that charmed me. He was a genuinely nice guy—easy to talk to and, best of all, he made me laugh.

I was so engrossed in Frank and his lively conversation that, at first, I didn't notice the commotion around us. Too late, I looked up just in time to see a flash of bare skin disappear around the corner of the building. Everyone around us had burst out laughing, pointing in that direction. Suddenly, I realized what I'd missed.

"My first streakers!" I gasped. I turned to Frank accusingly. "And I missed them because of *you!*"

Frank looked properly contrite. "Sorry. I'll get them to do it again."

I didn't think Frank was serious, but before I could say a word, he scrambled up from the ground and disappeared around the corner of the dorm. A few minutes later, I heard a peal of shrill laughter. I whipped my head around, and there they were: the two streakers, as naked as babes, running like mad demons down the span of lawn between dorms. The laughter intensified, and my eyes widened. A *third* streaker had joined the other two. He was tall and slender, with curly black hair and a moustache. Kind of Jim Croce-looking.

Oddly enough, Frank missed the whole thing, or so he said. He reappeared at my side a few minutes later as if nothing had happened.

"Thanks," I said drily. "You didn't have to go to so much trouble to impress me."

He shrugged. "Well, I couldn't let you miss your first streakers."

What could I say? He'd done it for *me*.

That was the beginning of our relationship. It's been thirty-nine years now, and we have two wonderful, grown children and two grandsons. Frank doesn't streak anymore, but that doesn't mean he's stopped getting naked. And I don't mean in the ordinary sense that we *all* get naked.

A few years ago, my sister, Kathy, was visiting, and she jokingly complained about the curtains in the guest room being too sheer. After she left, Frank said something about buying new curtains, and I brushed him off, insisting Kathy was overly sensitive, and the curtains were just fine.

"I'll prove it to you," Frank said, with a mischievous glint in his eye. "Give me a minute, then go out into the driveway and look up at the windows. *You* tell *me* if the curtains are too sheer."

I obediently headed outside into the darkness. When I got to the end of the driveway, I turned to look up at the guest windows—and my eyes widened. I began to laugh. I laughed so hard my knees buckled and tears began to stream down my face. I laughed so hard my belly ached, and I swear I almost peed my pants. (Actually, I think I *did* pee my pants…just a little.)

There, through the curtains, I saw my husband, buck-naked, jumping up and down on the bed like a five-year-old. Even as I type this, I've got tears in my eyes. Just the memory sends me cackling. That's my Frank. He always keeps me laughing.

My neighbors across the street didn't witness the antics of my husband that night, but they sure know about the story. It was too good not to share. (And guess what? He was right—the curtains *were* too sheer.)

I feel blessed that Frank walked into the clinic that day, and doubly blessed that I had the courage to sit down next to him at the party and strike up a conversation. And I never, ever forget what a lucky girl I am to have found the man of my dreams—one who is loving and supportive and fun and sweet. And who still makes me laugh! It works the other way, too.

A couple of weeks ago, while house-hunting in Myrtle Beach, we saw a home on a golf course and noticed it didn't have a fence to separate our yard from the fairway. As we drove away with our realtor at the wheel, Frank suggested we get a radio-activated pet-control system that administers a little shock through the dog's collar when he gets too close to the boundaries.

"Not only would it stop Cooper from going into the fairway," Frank said with a wry grin, "it would also stop golfers from coming into our yard."

I didn't get the joke. I thought about that a moment and then said in all seriousness, "But how would we get the golfers to wear the collar?"

Well, it's a good thing Frank wasn't at the wheel or he would've driven off the road. He and our realtor must have laughed for ten minutes straight. (I'm pretty sure our realtor, Steve, had tears in his eyes.)

I think laughter is one of the best recipes for a happy marriage. Maybe I'm just one of the lucky ones, but every day when I hear the garage door opening, I still feel a little flutter of excitement. My honey is home!

No matter which "first met" story I tell—the rather humdrum one about the flu shot or the fun one about the streaking incident, one thing is for sure. Frank *is* stuck on me.

And I'm stuck on Frank.

Carole Bellacera is the author of seven books of women's fiction. Her latest novel, *Lily of the Springs,* is the recipient of an Honorable Mention Award for Genre Fiction in the 2013 Writer's Digest Self-Published Book Awards. Her first novel, *Border Crossings,* a hardcover published by Forge Books, was a 2000 RITA® Award nominee for Best Romantic Suspense and Best First Book and for the 2000 Virginia Literary Award in Fiction. Carole's short fiction and non-fiction have appeared in magazines such as *Woman's World, The Star, Endless Vacation* and *The Washington Post.* In addition, her work has appeared in various anthologies such as Kay Allenbaugh's *Chocolate for a Woman's Heart, Chocolate for a Couple's Heart* and *Chicken Soup for Couples.*

Visit Carole online at www.carolebellacera.com.

Once Upon a Dream

Delilah Marvelle

Nothing ever came easy to me. I was one of those girls who always had to fight for everything I ever wanted in life, including respect. Looking back, I'm glad for it. It made me into who I am today, and more important, it tossed me straight into the arms of my incredible husband, Marc. Even though he and I met when I was only seventeen, let me preface by saying that at seventeen, I was actually closer to being forty at heart. It goes back to that whole nothing-ever-came-easy-to-me sort of thing.

When my father remarried, I soon found myself living with a stepmother who genuinely hated me for reasons I never understood. At the time, nobody knew my stepmother was bipolar. She hadn't been diagnosed. Well before any diagnosis, I knew something wasn't right. Locking a kid in a basement with no lights for hours at a time, shoving a kid down the stairs for punishment, beating a kid with the metal part of the belt until blood covered it were only some of the acts of physical and mental abuse I endured over the years. Growing up with a woman who lashed out at everyone and everything is what ultimately made me into a writer. I began seeing a different world beyond the fairy tales my real mother used to read to me as a child. It made me realize that evil stepmothers were, in fact, real. And they did a hell of a lot more than keep you from attending a ball. They kept you from believing in yourself. They also kept you from wanting more for yourself.

I firmly believe that you can't write about life if you haven't lived it. And the same applies to real love. Shortly before meeting my future husband, I was at a turning point in my life. I was starting my first year of college, and even though I wanted to get away from my family and the craziness and abuse it brought, I couldn't afford to live on my own. So I dealt with it. But I had a plan. One that didn't include a man. I believed the only person capable of bailing me out of the house was me, and I knew the only way to do it was by getting a few side jobs, saving money and getting a degree.

Destiny had other plans.

A girlfriend of mine invited me to her Halloween party. It was outside of town, and I didn't know anyone else who'd be attending. My options that night were to either study or to party. I'm usually a good girl capable of turning away parties during exams. Really. But for some reason, I felt like I needed to go. It was like my gut kept telling me that something incredible was about to happen. Yeah, I know. At a Halloween party. The writer in me ran with it.

I went into a vintage-clothing store and bought a black velvet dress and some old jewelry. Given my love for all things historical, I went as a Victorian vampire. I expected to meet new people and have a good time, but my gut feeling kept chewing away at me, telling me someone special was about to happen. I was going to meet someone. Someone meant for me.

The party was in full swing. The music was blaring. People were shouting over each other while eating. I met a lot of nice people, but as the night went on, I began to realize I had deluded myself into thinking that special someone would be walking into my life during a Halloween party. I've done it to myself before. It's that annoying hopeful sense of being ready to share your life with someone who will be there for you no matter what. As the night started coming to a close, I asked myself why the heck I had blown off studying for my exams for…well…nothing.

And then a small group of guys walked through the door. They were well over late, and they were damn proud of it. My gaze veered to one of them, and I'm telling you, my heart stopped. People say there's no such thing as love at first sight. My take on that? Pfft. Take a number. It's real.

He was beautiful. His dark brown hair hung into his amber eyes, and it was obvious he forgot to shave. His scruffy appearance didn't match the military Russian uniform he was wearing, and although the rest of the guys with him were loud and obnoxious, he had a quiet smile and soft-spoken tone. I couldn't keep my eyes off him. And neither could all the other girls around me.

Within minutes, he was surrounded, and I missed my chance to say hello. I spent the rest of the night watching him from a distance. I kept waiting for a chance to introduce myself. It never came.

Some people were starting to leave, and I decided to get something to eat. As I turned away from the food table with my mouth full of Doritos, I found him standing right behind me. He smiled, and every Dorito in my mouth turned to mush. He leaned in and started talking to me as if he'd been waiting to say hello himself all night.

I was never one to get nervous around guys, seeing as I grew up a tomboy and most of my friends *were* guys, but this guy—Marc—made me realize I was dealing with someone I'd met before. Someone I'd met with my heart. There's that Disney song from *Sleeping Beauty* called "Once Upon a Dream," and my mind was singing it. The more we talked, the more I realized how genuine he was. And how genuine my own reaction to him was. Yes, he was beautiful, but that wasn't what drew me in. What drew me in was the way he looked at me. It was as if I was the only person he was genuinely interested in getting to know. It made me feel special. And before I knew it, we were dancing together, laughing together and hanging out together as if we'd known each other our entire lives. We eventually exchanged numbers. And then he left.

I went home that night feeling something was different. It was an eerie feeling. Usually, when I crawled into bed, I felt like I had only myself and the stories I wrote in my head. I started writing a different story. A story about him and me. That same night, in my diary, I wrote the first thing that came into my head. I wrote: *I met the man I'm going to marry.* (Really. I did.)

Because we lived an hour apart from each other and the Internet didn't exist, we started writing weekly letters. I was always running to the mailbox, waiting for his next letter. He became the person I poured my soul out to. And soon, I began pouring out more than I'd ever shared with anyone. About my stepmother and how miserable she made my life. Marc reignited my belief in not only myself but the belief that good people not only really did exist, but that they deserved a happily ever after.

My stepmother, not to mention my own father, made it difficult for us to see each other. I think they began to realize how serious Marc and I were getting, and in their minds, it was a problem. They kept telling me I was moving too fast. They kept telling me I'd end up pregnant and that they'd kick me to the street for it. What they didn't realize was that, after everything I'd been through with them, their threats were meaningless. I was being genuinely loved by someone special. And I knew I had to cherish what I had found before my family broke it.

Even though I was only nineteen years old, I packed my stuff one night and took off with Marc to get married in Arizona, where some of his family was. It was the best thing I ever did. Nineteen years later, I'm still married to that soft-spoken man and have two awesome kids who make me believe that love at first sight is everything it should be: real.

Delilah Marvelle is the winner of *RT BOOK Reviews* Reviewer's Choice for Best Sensual Historical Romance of the Year. *Booklist* named her historical romance *Forever and a Day* a TOP 10 Romance of 2012. When she isn't writing, she's digging through historically inappropriate research books that make her poor husband blush.

You can visit her at her website at
www.delilahmarvelle.com
or her blog, which explores the
naughtier side of history, at
www.delilahmarvelle.blogspot.com.

A Leap of Faith Straight to the Altar

SONALI DEV

At sixteen I knew exactly who I was going to marry. At twenty-three I realized that wasn't how things were going to turn out. When it takes you your entire young adulthood to realize that your soul mate isn't, well, your soul mate, it's not exactly like you're heartbroken or anything. What you are is ready for a fresh start. Hungry for it, even. And bloody determined that this time your soul mate is going to snap in place against your half of your collective soul and stay there. And this time you're ready to do whatever it takes to make sure that the fit is tight and unbreakable. But that wasn't quite the answer I could give my parents, my grandparents, my aunts and uncles when they asked what exactly I was looking for. How do you tell those who changed your diapers and consequently earned the right to live vicariously through your youth that permanency, constancy, essentially a guarantee was what you were seeking, when "handsome, rich and smart" was so much more exciting, not to mention easier to look for.

It was hard enough to convince my friends and family that I, their little feminist, their perpetually soapbox-perched firecracker, was actually asking for help with seeking a husband. Growing up in India some twenty years ago, this was entirely normal in most families. But, while not entirely unheard of, arranged marriages weren't quite the norm in mine. My grandmother, who was one of the first "lady doctors" in post-colonial India, had married a man of her choosing and been banished from her home and family for her decision. My cousins and friends responded to the news that I was actually entertaining the thought of letting my parents look for a husband for me with an intervention, much like one they might have staged had I been on drugs. My mother's first reaction was to list all my friends who happened to be male as possible romantic interests. "What about X, he's a doctor and so handsome?" "What about Y, he's been sweet on you since tenth grade?"

But I was determined, even in the face of ominous warnings. "With your upbringing, you could never handle the male-dominated arranged-marriage scene!" (Yes, there is a scene.) And the shock. "Are you crazy? Why would you want to marry a man who can't find his own wife?" (Yes, the irony.) As for the male domination, in my startling naiveté I actually hoped for someone to demand a dowry so I could shut them down and teach them a thing or two. What was the point of doing something so very off-the-wall if I couldn't fight and fell a few social dragons along the way? As for the shock, well, how else was I going to meet men with the express guarantee that they were in it for the long haul?

But the naysayers had been right. The path to an arranged marriage wasn't exactly lined with exciting battles against dowry seekers, or with roses, for that matter. Unlike my mother, whose spectacular debut on the arranged-marriage scene resulted in my father wanting to sell his soul for her at first sight, I was paraded in front of a dozen men without quite the same results. Yes, I refused to do my hair or wear lipstick. Yes, I spoke my mind and showed them the me who was looking for unconditional acceptance, not the me who wanted to reel someone in and then reveal my full splendor, bit by bit (as advised, in all sincerity, by one of my aunts). What was the point of turning this most romantic quest for a soul mate into a transaction, if I couldn't at least be honest? Although in truth, I wanted what everyone saw as transactional to be romantic. I wanted a man to take one look at me, at my unbrushed hair, my unpainted lips, my unvarnished opinions, and love them enough to take the leap with me straight to the altar.

For the few months before the thirteenth man was set up for me to meet, every conversation I had with every human being I encountered inadvertently snaked its way to my Husband Search. "Has the click happened yet?" my grandmother asked with her hawk-eyed accuracy. "Have you decided to get off your high horse and adjust your expectations?" random relatives asked without having any idea what my expectations even were. "Are you ready to give up this madness?" my most loyal friends asked. To be honest, I was close. Of the twelve men I had considered, only one had come close to breaking my heart, which in itself was pretty darned heartbreaking, given that these men came highly recommended through my parents' impressive and extensive social network.

When my mother told me about Boy Number Thirteen ("boy," by the way, is what all marriageable men in India are called for reasons only a social anthropologist can explain), all I could do was groan. Thirteen was my last lucky number, one, eight, nine, and eleven already having passed without altering my half-souled state. My levels of hope were low, my backup plan in place—my GRE taken, my grad-school apps ready to go. I went running, mostly to torture my mother by being late. She'd taken to reading me my numbers every day. "It's been ten boys. Eleven. Good Lord, is he the thirteenth one already?" Nothing like an arranged marriage to complicate a perfectly healthy mother-daughter relationship.

When I arrived at my parents' country club to meet yet another potential soul mate, I was not just on my last remaining lucky number, I was on the last dredges of hope. I was also a good fifteen minutes late. My knee throbbed from having fallen during my run of rebellion, and the bottom of the loose salwar pants I had pulled on in a hurry had slipped over my foot and tangled in my shoe. I saw my future husband for the first time with my leg kicked up, in the middle of yanking my pants off my shoe, not to mention the unbrushed hair and the absence of lipstick. To this day, he insists he didn't notice, which pretty much sums up why my soul is still snapped tight into his after close to two decades. Who can resist a man who sees none of the madness that is you?

So here was this "boy," a good seven years older than me, down from America in want of a wife, not yet in possession of a fortune per se but in possession of a couple of master's degrees, and the hint of a dimple in one cheek. And an appetite. As we talked into the wee hours of morning, he proceeded to eat everything on the menu without a hint of self-consciousness. Being denied authentic Indian food in America will do that to you. And he laughed at everything I said. And he used an awful lot of the word "yes." As in, do you like to read? Yes. Do you like to travel? Yes. Movies? Yes. Music? Yes. My future swept up to greet me. I even remember the exact moment when I knew with absolute certainty that I was going to grow old with this man. The lamppost shone down on us as we sat leaning forward on our lawn chairs, empty plates strewn across our table, and he said something about his nephew and smiled the kind of smile that screamed "family over all else," and that dimple made an appearance.

Seven days after that, we were married.

But it almost didn't happen. He, in his all-American way, left me that night with an "I'll call you," which apparently was man-speak for "bye" and didn't have anything to do with an actual phone being picked up. So, when my mother asked if she should call his family as is the protocol in traditional arranged marriages, I informed her not to bother, because he was going to call (no, not even an arranged marriage can save you from the "will he call?" conundrum). This, of course, led his family to believe that I wasn't interested. That's what you get when you try to mooch off centuries-old tradition and mix it freely with the rules of modern-day dating. But thank God for the general bastardization of tradition. His mother threw protocol to the wind and, unlike her son, picked up the phone. And the precarious misunderstanding crumbled, revealing a fact every marriage must invariably learn to live with: a man's utter inability to communicate.

But what he lacked in terms of communication, he made up for in terms of enthusiasm. He showed up at my doorstep at five the next morning (very skillfully playing the jet-lag card) and whisked me off to breakfast and then to lunch and then to dinner. Somewhere in the course of that day, he asked me if I wanted to marry him. Amazingly enough, it wasn't a hard decision, especially not after he went down on one knee on the concrete floor of a parking lot in the middle of a power outage.

After eighteen years of marriage, I couldn't tell you why the decision was that easy. Maybe it was the fact that from the first time we met, every time someone asked him for a decision, he involved me in it. Maybe it was the fact that the way he looked at me when I dressed up to go out with him was exactly the way he looked at me when I pulled on my oldest T-shirt and shorts. Maybe it was the fact that our first act of intimacy was him resting his head on my lap. But, whatever it was, there was never a moment of discomfort with him. Never a moment of being strangers.

Maybe that's what they mean when they talk about soul mates. Because it couldn't possibly have anything to do with having common tastes and interests. In the years that have followed, we have disagreed on so much more than we've agreed on. He still says yes a lot, but it's mostly to get me off his back. His appetite, which I had found so very endearing, has been gobbled up by a fifteen-year-long health kick. And if you ask him to tell the story of how we met and married, you'd probably get an entirely different version. But when he talks about our nephews and nieces and our kids, his smile still screams "family over all else." I still don't brush my hair, and he continues to look at me the exact same way whether or not I do. And after all these years, if you sent me back in time and gave me not just thirteen but thirteen hundred "boys" to choose from, chances are I'd still choose the one who never felt like a stranger.

Sonali Dev writes Bollywood-style love stories that make a crazy tangle with her life as wannabe supermom and domestic goddess. Sonali lives in the Chicago suburbs with her very patient and often amused husband and two children who demand both patience and humor, and of course her characters who can't stop doing Bollywood dances inside her head. Sonali's debut novel, *A Bollywood Affair*, will be available from Kensington in November 2014.

Find her online at www.sonalidev.com.

Falling for My Husband

Jen McLaughlin

Okay, first things first. One thing you have to know about my husband is this: He's the least-clumsy person you'd ever meet. The man could fall down the stairs and land on his feet like a cat. It's ridiculous how non-clumsy he is. I often tease him for this, and he loves to make fun of me for being the complete opposite of agile—aka, a bit of a klutz. I admit this. But the fact that he is as smooth on his feet as he is?

Well, that makes the story of how we met even more interesting...

All right, now, picture this. I'm at a party, and it's dark outside. Drinks are flowing freely and people are chatting everywhere. You know, the way typical college-aged parties tend to be. Outside, there's a bonfire in the backyard, where most of the party is gathered. The makeshift bar is stationed in the kitchen, so people are going in and out nonstop.

Now, I've been to this house quite a few times, since I'm a close friend of the person who is throwing the party. Recently mixed drink in hand, I walk away from the kitchen and almost crash into this tall guy. He's just over six-foot, and I'm just over five-foot-one...and a half.

I've never seen him before, but he catches my attention immediately—as well as catching *me* so I don't hit the ground. I look up after I regain my balance. He has blond hair and blue eyes, and a smile that makes me hold my breath. Yep. I totally held my breath. Cliché and all.

We didn't really talk much at this point in time. I'm a little embarrassed at literally almost falling at this guy's feet, so I smile and kind of brush past him. I, of course, steal a look back at him, but then head outside. As I walk toward the bonfire, someone stops me to chat.

To this day, I don't even remember who it was, because my mind was still on *him*. The blond guy who'd caught me just moments before. By the time I finish chatting with this unremembered person (sorry, whoever you were), I'm ready to join the party again.

I sip my drink out of the red Solo® cup (college party, remember?) and head down the hill. After a second, I realize someone is in front of me. It's dark and I can't see who it is... but I know one thing...

He is walking *way* too fast.

It is black outside, so he can't see it, but he is about to hit the dip in the yard that is pretty darn deep. I reach out to try to stop him, but I am too late. He wipes out. Literally wipes out, flat on his butt, and slides down the hill. I stumble after him, trying to catch up, feeling awful for not catching him sooner.

"Are you okay?" I ask breathlessly, dropping to my knees at his side. It's not until I am this close that I realize it's *him*. The guy from the kitchen.

He laughs. "Yeah, I'm fine."

We both stand, and he brushes himself off. I just kind of stand there, being the awkwardly shy girl I've always been. He gives me a smile, the type that makes your heart do a flip-flop in your chest, and then heads off to his group of friends, while I head off to mine.

I didn't see him again all night long, so I figured that was the end of that.

Fast-forward to a few nights later. I am waitressing for some extra cash, and I am at work, watching the door for any signs of people coming in. It's deader than a doornail, I kid you not.

"Hey, I know you," someone says from behind me.

I'd been told there is a new guy starting, but not his name. I turn with a smile. The guy behind me is cute, blond, and has blue eyes. Something about him rings a bell, but I have no idea why or what. "I don't think so. I'm Jen."

We introduce ourselves, and then all night long we chat. He is a graduate of high school and is joining the Marines. He is leaving in August and has a girlfriend. I am a single mom to a baby—long story, there—and staying here. I have a crush on him, I'm not gonna lie, but he has a girlfriend. Case closed. Off-limits.

So, we do what we can do, under the circumstances. We become close friends.

This status lasts a long time. We met in the summer, and he left for boot camp that following August. We'll fast-forward a bit more now...

He comes back three months later, and we hang out as much as we can. He still has a girlfriend, and I have a boyfriend now, too. Still just friends. He leaves me again, this time heading off for basic training in North Carolina. He calls me every few weeks, just to chat and check in on me, but he is gone. And I miss him.

Skip forward to Christmas. The holiday comes around, and he stops by on Christmas Eve night. I have a boyfriend now, so I'm therefore unavailable, and I think he is, too...only, he tells me he isn't. His girlfriend broke up with him earlier in the month, and I hadn't even known about it until now. He stays late into the night, and we talk and talk for hours, just as we always do when we get together.

Again, the attraction between us is undeniable. It always is. But it never seems to work out between us, *darn it*. After all, I am still stuck in Pennsylvania, and he is now moving across the country to Washington state. You can't get much farther apart than that and remain in the US.

This is goodbye...again.

My heart breaks a little when I hug him for what I am sure is the last time.

He leaves, and I move on, as people tend to do.

Three months later, I get a phone call from an area code I don't recognize. I almost don't answer it. Almost let it go to voice mail. But something tells me to pick up the phone. So...I do. It is *him*. He is calling to tell me his duty station got changed, and he is now only four hours away, as opposed to a whole country away, and he is coming home that weekend.

We make plans to get together for dinner, but I never dream anything is going to happen because of it. We've been going out to eat together for almost a year now. What makes this time any different? Nothing.

But then we see each other, and for the first time ever? We are *both* single.

I still remember the way my heart sped up when he picked me up that day. The three of us go out to our favorite restaurant—him, me and my daughter—and we talk for hours. Then, after she goes to bed, he sits down on the couch and we snuggle up to watch a movie.

We get to talking about his breakup with his girlfriend and discuss my life and my singleness—*ahem*—before we both just...fall silent.

As if in slow motion, his mouth descends to mine, and the second we kiss, I just know...this is it. This is the man I've been waiting for my whole life. He might not live locally, and he might be a Marine, which is a pretty unpredictable life, but I've been friends with him for over a year now.

This. Is. It.

I know so much about him already, and now I have the chance to find out even more.

I don't hesitate. I take the chance I've been given.

Looking back over thirteen years later...we had a rocky start, since we got together right before the World Trade Center got hit by two airplanes, and the world kind of exploded. His job as a Marine introduced a whole new kind of fear into my life, but I wouldn't have ever walked away from a second of those fears, changes, and heartbreaks.

All of it added up to be what we are now. We've been married for over eleven years, and we have four beautiful children together. We've moved across the country, moved back, gotten out of the Marines, changed career fields. We've loved. We've lost. We've fought.

But one thing never changed....

Our love and commitment to one another.

And it never will.

Jen McLaughlin is a *New York Times*, *USA Today* and *Wall Street Journal* best-selling author. She writes steamy, best-selling New Adult books for the young and young at heart. Her first release, *Out Of Line*, came out September 10, 2013. It hit both the *New York Times* and *USA Today* lists within the first week of release. She also writes best-selling contemporary romance under the pen name Diane Alberts.

Visit her online at www.dianealberts.com/jen-mclaughlin.

Once in a Blue Moon

Deanna Raybourn

They say true love comes along once in a blue moon. And a butterfly can conjure a hurricane a thousand miles away, changing history and landscapes with just a flutter. Personal history can be bewitched by things just as inconsequential. A train not taken, an appointment changed, a door opened a second too late, and events unfold differently, like a map whose contour lines have shifted. If you step off a curb at just the wrong moment, you could be mowed down by a city bus. Or you could be mowed down by love, moving so fast that everything becomes a blur—an Impressionist painting of the life you thought you knew.

    I was nineteen years old when I met my husband in a place I wasn't even supposed to be. I was a sophomore in college and looking for any excuse to ditch my political science class. "Then come to my communications class instead," said my friend. "There's a guy in there you just need to see, he's *that* cute." A chance to see a beautiful boy or an hour of my professor droning on about municipal administration? It wasn't even close. I grabbed a soda from the vending machine and followed her in. I don't remember anything about the instructor or what she talked about. Was she even a she? I can't recall. But I remember the first time I saw him. He was sitting in the front, and I had to walk past him to throw away my soda can. When I chucked it into the trash can, he looked up at me with the most beautiful blue eyes I'd ever seen and said, "You know, you really ought to recycle your aluminum."

It was the single-worst pickup line I'd ever heard. And all he got in trade for it was a smile. I didn't say a word, but I memorized those eyes. I tried to place the color in nature. Forget-me-nots? A blue morpho butterfly? A summer horizon? A few years later, as I stood on a Caribbean beach watching the sea change under a December sky, I finally found their match. I've seen those eyes laughing, and very, very occasionally, I've seen them fill with tears. I've seen them on camera, when the light catches them so strikingly they seem almost iridescent. And still, just as on that first day, they have the power to move me to distraction.

After that first brush with serendipity, we kept running into each other on campus. And every time, he stuck his foot firmly in his mouth, wedging it there immovably. He saw me wearing a dress one day—a big departure from my usual jeans and high-tops—and looked me over, smiling. "You look great. What's the occasion?" he asked. I held my answer for the length of a heartbeat. "I'm going to a funeral."

A less stalwart soul might have given up after that. But he was Galahad, armor polished, firmly mounted, quest undertaken. Nothing deterred him. Neither disappointment nor discomfort discouraged him. He charged on, into the fire, time after time. Was I the dragon or the grail? Opponent or prize? Was he looking to vanquish me or carry me off in triumph? I don't think I ever really knew, and the not knowing was part of the intoxication. And intoxicated I was, drunk off the thought of him. A glimpse of him across campus would hold me for days, days that I counted in skipped heartbeats.

Some weeks after the funeral conversation, he had managed to get my number. I never knew how. He gathered his courage and called me up at half past six on a weekend, an Arthurian knight with call waiting. As soon as I answered, he asked, his tone smooth as molten caramel, "What's a girl like you doing home on a Saturday night?" I almost didn't have the heart to tell him the truth. But I must have been the dragon after all. A grail would never have been cruel enough to say with finality, "I'm getting dressed to go out." He withdrew graciously, ceding the field. A strategic retreat while he considered his next tactic.

The following week was the university luau, a party I was dreading. I had moped and mooned, certain I had overplayed my hand. I dreaded the idea of forced Polynesian fun, and worst of all, I knew the boy with the beautiful blue eyes wouldn't be there. He hated organized frivolity. But my mother, speaking wisdom, insisted I go. "You'll have fun," she promised. "You never know what's going to happen." So in defiance of my wretched mood, I tied on a grass skirt and went, hopes fluttering near the ground like small, wingless things. As soon as I walked in, I saw him—unexpectedly, wonderfully *there* where I least anticipated finding him. He had come with his best friend, and the moment he spotted me, his eyes dilated in pleasure. I went to him. I spent the evening dancing with the boy with the beautiful blue eyes and his best friend. I discovered many months later that they argued over who would ask me out, tallying up old scores to see who had earned the advantage. The blue eyes won.

When the time finally came and he asked me out, by my calculations I owed him at least one date for all the humiliation he'd suffered, all the thorns he'd overcome, pricking his pride in small, unfatal wounds. Would I have said yes as easily if he hadn't managed to pitch wide of the plate with every pickup line he'd thrown my way? Probably not. It was the faltering that hinted at gentleness under the coolly arrogant façade. He swaggered when he walked, but his eyes told an entirely different tale. Those eyes talked about hopes unrealized, dreams unshared. He longed for something. I closed my eyes and imagined he smelled of crushed four-leaf clovers and broken wishbones, cold candles on a birthday cake, a rabbit's foot rubbed bare. A river of deep, dark sweetness ran like molasses under his skin and seeped out of him, wafting behind him as he walked. I watched other girls as they sniffed after him, chasing it, hungering for the sugary promise. But he never looked around. He walked with those remarkable eyes fixed straight ahead, seeing right through them as if they weren't even there. They were insubstantial as ghosts to him, and the only thing that was real was the promise of what he had always been looking for.

For our first date, he left a bouquet of blue irises on my seat in the car for me to discover rather than bringing them to the door. There was subtlety in his wooing. Irises were beloved of perfumers, the emblem of French kings. They were my favorite flower at the time, an unexpected choice that told me he paid attention when I talked. An actor, he took me to the theater. It was an invitation into his world, a stepping stone to his dreams. The play was *King Lear*, and when the blood ran freely, I hid my face, glad he'd chosen something violent instead of romantic. I didn't want to watch others kiss when all I could think about was kissing him. We went to dinner afterward, and as I stared down at my empty plate, I realized I had been able to eat with him, something I had never before managed on a first date. *It's a sign*, something within me whispered. *How can you spend forever with a man if you can't even eat around him?* Sometimes my subconscious is alarmingly prosaic. Every other first date had seen me choke down a few reluctant mouthfuls, pleading a big lunch, while the butterflies in my stomach flew like acrobats. But not this time. This time, with him, I ate ravenously, filling myself with all the possibility that simmered between us.

Three weeks later, under a blue moon, he told me for the first time that he loved me, and he worked all that summer, sweating under a hot Texas sun cutting grass to earn the money to buy me an engagement ring. I said yes to a boy I hadn't even known five months before—terrified, but more certain than scared. We married two years later—on the day I graduated from college. I was frightened to marry that young, but underneath the fear, I recognized something else—the absolute inevitability of him. So many little twists in the path had led us to each other. If either of us had taken a single wrong turn, we would never have met. But the butterfly wings brushed against fate and, in that perfect storm of destiny, we happened.

It has been twenty-five years since that day I saw him sitting in a place I wasn't supposed to be. When I have been nervous about our future, he has been our rock, the immovable object to my irresistible force. My fears and worries are flights of fancy—they've danced around him, occasionally ruffling his hair, but never pushing him off the path. His certainty has been breathtaking, his absolute confidence in us unshakeable. Once, I asked him how he was so sure of us when I had been so uncertain. The face with the beautiful blue eyes smiled at me and said, "Because I wished for you." And everyone knows that wishes made on blue moons always come true.

A sixth-generation native Texan, *New York Times* bestselling author Deanna Raybourn graduated from the University of Texas at San Antonio with a double major in English and history and an emphasis on Shakespearean studies. Deanna's novel *Silent in the Grave* won both a RITA® and *Romantic Times* Reviewers' Choice Award. Her Lady Julia Grey series has been nominated for an Agatha, three Daphne du Mauriers, a Last Laugh, four additional RITAs, and two Dilys Winns, among other awards. Her latest novel, *A Spear of Summer Grass*, chronicles the adventures of a scandalous flapper in 1920s Kenya. Deanna makes her home in Virginia where she lives with her husband and daughter. *City of Jasmine*—a 1920s adventure novel—will release March 2014.

Visit Deanna online at www.deannaraybourn.com.

Love at First Sight?

Caryn Moya Block

I've had several people ask me why I have *destined* mates in my paranormal romance stories. Some of them even scoff at the idea and complain that real life isn't like that. I would have to disagree. I think it can be like that, and here is why.

When I attended college in Arizona, one of my professors asked me to be a part of the new student government they were trying to get organized. I agreed and dived in wholeheartedly, writing bylaws and having elections. Then I was invited to attend the statewide student government conference, and again, I agreed. Little did I know that by doing so I would find the man I was going to marry.

Our college had three different campuses in three different cities, all about thirty-five miles apart. Each campus had its own student government with members attending the conference. To save money, the school decided we would all meet at the main campus (not mine) and ride up together to the conference with our advisor.

A longtime girlfriend and I drove up together and parked at the main campus. Neither of us had been there before, and we didn't really know our way around. We decided to head for the office and hoped someone there would tell us where to meet the rest of our group.

I will never forget the next few moments. We had turned down the proper pathway that ran to the office when a young man came out of the door and started walking toward us. His blond curly hair was down to his shoulders, and he wore a T-shirt and a pair of ratty jean cutoffs. Seeing him was so overwhelming that I stopped. I *knew* from that *first moment* that this was the man I was going to marry.

"Who is that?" I asked my friend.

She replied that he was the president of the student government on this campus and would be leading our college group at the conference. My future husband walked up and started directing us to where we would be picking up our bus.

How did I *know* he was the one? I would say now that I was guided by the divine. At the time, I had no idea why I knew. I just did. It was like a voice spoke in my head: *There he is, the man I am going to marry.*

Was it love at first sight? No, it was *knowing* at first sight.

My husband of more than thirty years is a handsome man, but he isn't drop-dead gorgeous. It certainly wasn't his ratty clothes that drew me. Did I mention he had a goatee? With his sun-lightened blond hair, the goatee looked like a ball of lint and did nothing for him. In fact, the goatee covered up the cute dimple in his chin that I came to love later on.

Once we were all loaded onto the bus, I found out how wicked his sense of humor was and still is. One of the students was an older woman who was near my mother's age. She was a member of the student government from the third campus, and I had never met her before. As we were driving past the farms and pastures full of cows, somehow the fact they were different colors came up.

I sat quietly in my seat, amazed, while my future husband convinced the woman that white cows have white meat, dark cows have dark meat, and mixed-color cows are for hamburger.

I didn't know whether to be angry or laugh. I was taught to treat your elders with respect, and playing this prank on someone who could be my mother was unsettling. On the other hand, how was it she believed the bunk he was telling her? To say that my husband can be persuasive is a given.

Did we fall for each other immediately? No. In fact, he decided to make a play for my girlfriend during the conference. She wasn't interested, *thank goodness*, because she had a boyfriend waiting for her at home.

Just getting him to notice me took awhile. But I was determined, because in my heart, I *knew* he was the one. There was never a question in my mind that we were meant to be together.

Our courtship was rocky. We lived in different cities and literally had a mountain range between us. Luckily for me, student government business often had us on the phone with each other. Frequently, after school business was discussed, we would talk and learn more about each other. I started going to his baseball games, and he came down for our campus' picnic. Things became more serious when we started going steady.

At the next year's statewide student government conference, my future husband proposed. We had fallen head over heels in love. The road was still rocky when my parents didn't approve and my fiancé decided to join the Air Force after graduation. But we kept trying and working to be together.

August 1, 1981, we were married in a park in Arizona located on the Colorado River in front of our family and friends. My girlfriend stood up with me as my maid of honor, while our student government advisor was my fiancé's best man.

We have been together through thick and thin ever since, traveling around the world while my husband was in the Air Force and having two boys who are now adults. And it all started "*at first sight.*"

This last September, our first grandchild, Vera, was born. I can't wait to tell her about the first time I saw her grandpa walking toward me.

Love at first sight has always been an interest of mine. I will often ask other couples how they met. I know two other couples, both married more than thirty years, wherein the woman *knew* her future husband was the one. I am sure there must be more. Call it "love at first sight" or "knowing at first sight," but it isn't as rare as you would think.

In my romance novels, I write that my heroes and heroines may *know* at first sight that they are destined to be together. But it's never that easy for them. Just as my husband and I did, they will have to work at being together and learn to appreciate their perfect mate.

Caryn Moya Block burst onto the paranormal romance scene with *Alpha's Mate* in January 2012. Since then she has been an Amazon best seller, was named one of the Indie Authors to Watch in April 2012 by iReader Review and won the Global E-book Award for contemporary romance in 2012.

Visit her online at
www.carynmoyablock.com.

Falling in Love with the Intern

Megan Frampton

It was pre-Clinton, I didn't wear a blue dress, and he wasn't particularly besotted by my position.

But, other than that, the truth is that I dated, fell in love with, and eventually married my intern.

If it were in a novel, it'd be way too cliché to be believed. It was New York City in the late eighties. There were nights in clubs seeing seminal bands. We had completely different romantic pasts, different backgrounds, and it was meant to be a one-night stand.

Now it's close to twenty-five years later, and we're still together. Married. With a teenaged son.

We met for the first time at a Nick Cave concert at the Ritz in New York City. He was the music director of a local college radio station, and I was out of college by a few years and was the editor at a music industry tipsheet. A mutual friend introduced us because she knew he was interested in interning at my magazine.

We were both with other people at the time. I was in a long-dysfunctional relationship from college, while he had Quite the Reputation as being a ladies' man at his college. (As I found out later, his Reputation was Quite Deserved.)

The first time we met, or so he later told me, I wouldn't look at him, and he could barely hear me, because I was so shy and soft-spoken, plus we were at a rock show, so it was hard to hear anyway.

It's a classic office romance, when you look at it. He did join the magazine as an intern, and it got to be a habit for the two of us to go out for frozen yogurt when he was answering phones. I admired his very long legs in his very snug jeans, and he seemed to like making conversation with me. We were both with other people, but there was definitely a spark of...*something*.

Nothing happened while he was working for me, but eventually I was out of the long-dysfunctional relationship and had moved to my own apartment in Brooklyn. I was throwing a housewarming party and happened to be at CBGB's record canteen when I ran into him. He told me he'd broken up with his girlfriend. I handed him a party invite, and that was that.

And then—then he showed up at the party, coming all the way from New Jersey. He brought moonshine for his white-trash background and Jameson for my Irish heritage. We drank, and eventually he leaned into the fridge to grab something, and I grabbed his ass.

That might have been the bravest and stupidest thing I'd ever done.

We spent the rest of the party making out.

The next morning, I was mortified. Just like any romance heroine would be when she had done something so totally unlike herself. I'd just gotten out of a six-year relationship with the wrong guy, and what was I doing sucking face with some college guy who was younger than I am, lived in another state, and had been my intern?

If it hadn't worked out, that might have ended up being the Most Mortifying Experience of My Life. Thankfully, it did work out.

The next afternoon, he called. Just to make sure I was feeling all right. We talked for a while, and then—oh my God, we made plans to see each other.

What was I doing?

I was being adventurous. I was taking a risk, where I never had before, not romantically, not anywhere in my life. Even moving to New York City and taking a job at a music magazine hadn't been a particular risk. My free-spirited parents had raised me to follow my passion, and my passion was music. Not the making of it, mind you. I liked writing about it. My dad was a journalist who worked in the arts section, so it made some sense for me to do the same. Making a decent living was perhaps seventh on the list of things to strive toward, after Never Drink Inferior Beer, Stay Warm, and Wear Black All the Time. Things I continue to work toward.

Our first official date, we met at Sbarro underneath Madison Square Garden. I spilled my soda all over the floor. I was that nervous. He thought it was cute, not clumsy.

We talked on the phone. A lot. He was in the midst of finals during his senior year in college. He went to school in New Jersey, and I lived in Brooklyn. I'm not sure that it would have lasted if we had been able to see each other more. As it was, we were able to get to know each other via conversation rather than rushing headlong into a passionate affair.

I was still reeling from the six-year relationship breakup, and he was—at this time—already dating two women. Busy guy! (Again, quite deserving of his Reputation!) But we found we had a lot in common, beyond the fact that we'd shared mouth space a few weeks prior.

We were both English majors. We loved puns. We knew a lot about music and liked some of the same groups. We liked seeing live bands. We had the same political leanings. We knew the corporate job path wasn't for us. We were loyal. We both liked basketball and watching *Soul Train* on Saturday mornings. We were having fun getting to know one another.

If I hadn't taken that risk, if I hadn't asked myself, *What's the worst that happens? You hang out with a guy who isn't right for you who is very nice to look at? Maybe you get kissed a lot? That's not so bad*, I wouldn't have become the person I am today, with the man I'm married to, with a fabulous kid. I would have stayed safe, not taken risks—and not grabbed his ass.

Perhaps the lesson of my life shouldn't be "grab that ass," but then again, maybe it's the best advice I can offer.

Megan Frampton writes historical romance under her own name and romantic women's fiction as Megan Caldwell. Her Megan Frampton title, *What Not to Bare*, was one of Barnes and Noble's books that are "too sexy to read in public." She likes the color black, gin, dark-haired British men, and huge earrings, not in that order. She lives in Brooklyn, NY, with her husband and son.

Visit her online at
www.meganframpton.com.

Crossing the Pond

Mary B. Rodgers

MARY: Simon and I met in September of 2011 at the Stone Street Oyster Festival in New York City, on one of those cool, sun-drenched fall days when the sky is a perfect cobalt blue and the air so clear that you feel like you can see into outer space.

It was a setup job by a mutual friend, so I didn't get my hopes up. On my way there I became lost amid the tangle of Lower Manhattan's ancient and distinctly un-gridlike layout of streets. After a good half hour of frustration, I emerged out of yet another dead-end alleyway and found a string of bored cops watching a small protest march. Much later, I realized that protest marked the beginning of the Occupy Wall Street movement.

With great assurance, the cops pointed me in precisely the wrong direction from where I needed to go.

SIMON: The exact same thing happened to me!

MARY: I found the festival soon after and met up with my friends for a boozy afternoon of fried oysters and Prosecco.

Eventually, we moved up Stone Street to the venerable Harry's Bar, and Simon showed up. I definitely thought he was cute, and as our conversation shifted easily from a discussion of pop music to parsing social justice themes in our favorite books, I realized that he was very bright as well.

SIMON: She was smitten, of course.

MARY: Well, not yet—

SIMON: I thought she was very pretty and charming.

MARY: Simon was living in London at the time. He'd spent thirteen years working in New York but had decided to return to his home country for a while.

We began a fairly lively e-mail correspondence that culminated with me flying over to visit for a week in November. I rented a cute flat in Notting Hill, figuring that if Simon turned out to be a jerk, hell, I was in London! I was bound to have a good time.

SIMON: I'll have you know I was a perfect gentleman.

MARY: Toward the end of my stay, we spent a passion-filled night together at his flat, and I had the great pleasure the next morning of having a beautiful man cook me breakfast. I should add that he was naked at the time. I was sipping a cup of tea and ended up wearing most of it, despite my determined efforts to seem cool. Smitten as I was by his—

SIMON: Masculine splendor!

MARY: Masculine…really, darling?

SIMON: (nodding vehemently) I think that should be the running theme here—

MARY: Of course you do. Anyway, we began a trans-Atlantic courtship between London and Manhattan. Prior to that I'd considered Brooklyn long-distance, so this was something of an adjustment. But as the months ticked by, our relationship deepened. And in December of 2012, Simon asked me to move to England to be with him.

It was a big ask. I'd have to leave my friends, my family and my beloved New York City behind, and make a life for myself in a different country. But I'd never felt about anyone the way that I felt about Simon, and I've always believed that if you reach a point in your life when you won't take a chance on a new adventure, you might as well stop living altogether.

So even though I felt like I was about to leap off the edge of a precipice, I gathered my courage, took a deep breath...and jumped.

Several months after I arrived in London, Simon took me on a hike up the very steep Bunster Hill in Dovedale, a gorgeous area in the English countryside distinguished by glacier-carved valleys, clear, fast-running rivers and thickets of impossibly tall ancient oak trees. I'd had a cold for a while and was operating at about fifty-percent lung capacity, so a climb that would have been strenuous on my best day required a Herculean effort to complete.

SIMON: In my defense, I really had no idea at that point just how ill she still felt...

MARY: I thought it was another guy test, to see how "cool" I was, so I wasn't about to admit defeat. There I was, wheezing like a dying accordion on the top of a windswept mountain, early spring flowers just coming into bloom, the hills echoing with the bleating of baby lambs—I mean, I did appreciate the romance of it all, despite my lack of oxygen.

SIMON: And I went down on one knee and proposed.

MARY: It came as a complete surprise. Of course I said yes.

Simon and I had both promised ourselves that when we found the right person, we'd have a proper church wedding. But the vagaries of the British visa system dictated a swifter timeline. A few weeks after Simon proposed, we were married at the local town hall with my stepmother and his best friend as our witnesses.

Despite our unhappiness with the accelerated timetable and the lack of ceremony involved in the civil service, we both found ourselves tearing up as we held hands and repeated our vows. It turned out to be a very special day. We spent the remainder of the afternoon basking in the sunshine outside a local pub, quaffing bottle after bottle of champagne. And we comforted ourselves by setting plans in motion to have the church wedding for which we'd always hoped by the end of the year.

Simon and I are born "doers." Since I've been in London, our life together has been characterized by a mutual restlessness and sense of adventure. Weekends are for exploring and hiking and boating, not sleeping in.

Thus far, we've been on numerous walks on the Thames Path, rowed an old-fashioned wooden skiff on the river all the way from Richmond to Hampton Court—

SIMON: "We" rowed? Ahem. I believe that I performed the lion's share of work on that one—

MARY: I was steering! A very important job. And drinking wine.

SIMON: Also very important.

MARY: Indeed. I suppose it would have helped if either of us had paid attention to the tide table that day. We were no more than a half mile away from the Richmond Bridge Boathouse when the river turned against us. As it happened, this was a "king" tide, the highest tide of the year, which occurs when the sun, moon and Earth are closest in alignment. It's also the most powerful.

By the time we made it to the bridge right next to the boathouse, Simon was rowing so hard against a rushing wall of water that the skiff was practically standing on end.

SIMON: Lesson learned…

MARY: In less-strenuous pursuits, we've also played on the silk white sands of Camber Beach in Rye, strolled through the Jardin du Luxembourg in Paris, swum in crystal-clear coves in Ibiza, cheered mightily for the rowers at the Henley Royal Regatta, listened to world-class musicians play at the Royal Albert Hall, sampled the latest vintages at England's oldest winery and haunted countless charming pubs from Hammersmith to Waterloo.

And in the time that I've been here, I wrote another novel, *Project Catchstar*, a contemporary thriller featuring a funny, kick-butt heroine and a dashing Special Ops love interest.

SIMON: (preening) I assume that I was the model for said love interest?

MARY: But, of course, darling. Who else?

Simon is incredibly supportive of my writing. I trust him completely, so much so that he is the first person to see even my earliest, most embryonic drafts.

It's not that he gives me endless accolades or soft-pedals his criticism. I trust him because he is honest in his opinions and genuinely interested in my work. Writing can be a lonely endeavor even at the best of times. I'm incredibly fortunate to have a loving husband who is my most passionate advocate. I didn't think I'd ever find someone like Simon.

I look forward every day to continued warmth, laughter and new adventures with my own real-life romance hero.

A career performer and storyteller, Mary Rodgers was the keyboardist and lead vocalist in an all-female rock band for a number of years and has acted in leading roles in plays and musicals across the United States. Her first screenplay, *Common Ground*, won a finalist slot in the 2008 Moondance International Film Festival competition, and she is a member of the Screen Actors Guild/AFTRA and the New York chapter of Women in Film and Television. *Project Catchstar*, her New Adult action-adventure romance debut, released in December 2013.

Visit Mary online at www.mary-rodgers.com.

Thanks to Uisce Beatha (Water of Life)

Kat Simons

When I moved to Dublin, Ireland, in 1997 to do my PhD in animal behavior, I was twenty-six years old, never getting married, writing romance novels, and wondering how on earth people actually met in real life. Romance novels always have these clever meet-up situations for contemporary stories, but I had no idea how people really met their mates. I was curious for the sake of my writing, though, not for my own personal efforts, because I wasn't interested in having a relationship.

For the record, I wasn't avoiding marriage because I had anything against the institution. I write romance. I do like romance and love and marriage and all that stuff. I just didn't see it happening for me. I never wanted to invest my time in someone else's schedule. In the years before moving to Ireland, I had had a total of one two-month relationship. That was it. Nothing longer. Nothing more serious. I was okay with that because I wasn't looking for anything more.

I've just never been good at relationships. You know how women supposedly *want* a man to call the next day, say, after that first date or first meet-up? Not me. I usually wanted him *not* to call. And would you believe the bastards always called? It's like inadvertent reverse psychology.

Anyway, I *ran* from anything that might get serious and any man who wanted more from me than one night. I didn't like to be beholden to anyone else. I wanted to do with my time what I wanted and not be subjected to another person's demands. Time has always been my most valuable commodity, and I wasn't prepared to spend that commodity on a man. So I avoided commitment.

My mother wasn't the least surprised to find out I'd started to lean away from a permanent relationship. I was more interested in travel, writing, friends, science, everything else there was to do in life. Thankfully, I have an artist mother who was good with this. Not having to deal with any nagging to "settle down" really helps when one has decided not to settle down.

Moving to Ireland was an adventure designed to enjoy the country, get my advanced degree, see a new place and meet new people. But I didn't actually think I'd date much.

While my mother and I were hunting for a place for me to live in Dublin, a taxi driver warned me that I should be careful or I'd end up married to an Irishman. The comment was greeted by a lot of laughter on our part. This was *so* not happening. At least, not to me.

The *dadada* of the inevitable reversal of expectations practically booms here, doesn't it?

I looked around for about a week and finally found a room in a house share. The house was a large Georgian place in Dun Laoghaire (pronounced duhn leery; don't get me started on Irish spellings). In the upstairs part of the house, there were seven separate rooms for seven people. When I moved in, there were two other women and four men. In the basement of the house, our landlord lived with his wife and two young kids.

Living in a mixed house was great fun. The people changed over the years, though a few were there the entire time I lived in the house. Everyone was really nice and easy to get along with—most of the time. We each had our own rooms over three floors, then shared two bathrooms, a sitting room and a kitchen that was just off the sitting room. The house was near the Dun

Laoghaire pier so I had a view of the Irish Sea from my room and an excellent place to go for walks.

We managed to keep the peace in the house really well, too. The landlord came upstairs and did our dishes or tidied when things got out of hand, so we never had to have that fight. The place was freezing in the winters, so we all hung out in the sitting room in front of the heater, watching whatever we could get on TV. Every once in a while, we'd play games or go drinking together. We even had the occasional party. It was a cozy arrangement. If you wanted to talk, there was almost always someone around to visit with. If you wanted to be alone, you had your bedroom to disappear in. I couldn't have found a more perfect place to live as a newbie to Ireland.

For the first six months, I was the odd man out, being an American. Everyone else was Irish, though from very different parts of Ireland—which meant I had to get used to a host of different accents! They accepted me in, despite this, and never once made me feel uncomfortable or like a stranger. Then a guy from Scotland moved in, and we both got to be the foreigners in the house. When his friends from Scotland came over for a visit and met with the thicker-Irish-accented members of the house, I ended up acting as a translator because, to me, they all sounded strange.

I was living in the house for three weeks before I met the man who lived in the room on the ground floor. I walked into our sitting room late one night, and he was stretched out on the couch watching sports. We said a passing hello, and I walked into the kitchen, closing the door behind me. Then I hemmed. The guy on the couch was cute. And he looked tall! I have a particular soft spot for tall men. I'm tall-ish and have trouble feeling delicate and feminine with men smaller than I am. Personal bias I'm not proud of, but there you go. My men have to be tall.

The ground-floor guy and I exchanged passing pleasantries off and on as I started my PhD fieldwork. I flirted a bit, but not seriously—and I've never been sure if he realized I was flirting with him. He's the strong, silent type, so he's really hard to read.

We did get along well, and I liked sitting with him and talking. We didn't have a lot in common outwardly. He was into sports. I had a passing interest but wasn't a sports fanatic. I loved to read. He was mostly a newspaper and magazine guy who'd only just started to read books. He was an accountant. I was a scientist and a writer. He actually had a job and made money. I was a poor college student just starting to rack up my student loans. I was outdoorsy and had grown up with pets. He loved cities and had never owned so much as a goldfish. I'm a card-carrying pagan. He's a Mass-going Catholic.

If we'd been signed up on one of the online dating sites, we would *never* have been put together.

But our seeming lack of common interests didn't matter to me at the time. I wasn't looking for anything to really happen between us. I definitely wasn't on the hunt for a boyfriend. I was just flirting with a cute guy and thoroughly enjoying my new life in Ireland. Besides, he was my housemate, and hooking up with someone I lived with would complicate the living arrangement. I was nothing if not keen on avoiding complications in my life.

In the meantime, I was out most days watching deer in the Phoenix Park, wearing canvas trousers, wellies, and an oversized coat, layered up with sweaters, scarves and gloves to stay warm. Not exactly an attractive look. (On a side note, because of the size of my coat and my height, I was often mistaken for a man out in the field until people got close enough to see my face. See, not a very feminine look I had going.) There was no makeup, my hair was often tied up in a bun, and after the fieldwork, I mostly lounged around in pajamas—not the sexy type, either.

At one point in September, ground-floor guy came home from work in a mood and wanting a drink. He asked which of us housemates wanted to help him make a dent in the bottle of whiskey he'd gotten as a present. I was happy to help—I like a good glass of Irish whiskey—and another of the guys who happened to be around sat down with us, too. The bottle was opened, the first glasses consumed, and then the other housemate went out to the pub—leaving me and ground-floor guy to finish the bottle of whiskey.

Which we did.

When our housemate got home, he caught us making out on the living room couch. His reaction was to get all mushy and give us both big hugs, which was hilarious and made the whole thing fun instead of weird.

The next day, as was usual for my commitment-shy self, I backed way away from the situation. Ground-floor guy and I decided to stick to being just friends as we were housemates and didn't want to make things uncomfortable. And that was that.

For about two weeks.

Another weekend night, another bottle of whiskey, and another make-out session confirmed we weren't going to stop hooking up just because we were living in the same house. In fact, from my perspective, if we hadn't been housemates, I would have run away (as I was wont to do), and we never would have gotten together again. I can honestly say that I'm married now because the man I married just happened to be my housemate and I couldn't avoid him.

It helped that he was really cute and tall and for some reason still found me attractive even when wearing wellies and an oversized coat.

During my fieldwork, we continued to get together on Friday nights, but we didn't have our first real date until the fieldwork was over. Fieldwork involved me leaving the house at 5:30 A.M. to be in the park before sunrise and not getting home until usually 7 P.M. or later, depending on the bus schedule. For our first date, he took me to see *The Full Monty*, a movie about blue-collar workers in England doing a strip show to make money and deciding to do "the full monty," or taking everything off, to make their show different from any other. The movie was fantastic, funny, poignant, and about ordinary men stripping. I mean, really. Brilliant!

I knew I adored the man who took me to that kind of movie on a first date. Adored him enough to change my behavior and not run away.

A lot more happened to get us to marriage. There were ups and downs to our relationship, and a lot of us learning to find common ground (he's a mad reader now, and we have an extensive library of books; I regularly go to, and enjoy, sporting events). In fact, after almost twelve years of marriage, two kids, and two countries, there continue to be ups and downs. But we still find a way to stay strong together. We talk. We've learned to like each other's interests, and at a base level, it turns out we had a lot in common. We take each other as we are with no unreasonable expectations. And we're still in love.

At our wedding dinner, his best man got up and regaled the audience—including my parents!—with the story of how we met and how we got together. I was a little embarrassed, but how could I regret any of it? I'd somehow stumbled onto the man of my dreams without realizing it, expecting it, or even knowing it at the time. That taxi driver was right. Who knew? An Irishman did marry me.

All thanks to a bottle of whiskey and that big Georgian house in Dun Laoghaire.

Kat Simons earned her PhD in animal behavior, and then brought her knowledge to her paranormal romances, where she delights in taking nature and turning it on its ear. After traveling the world, she now lives in New York City with her family.

For more on Kat's books, visit her at www.katsimons.com.

Speeding Down the Relationship Super Highway*

Hope Tarr

When you meet Mr. Right, or Ms. Right as the case may be, odds are it will be nowhere near the movie magical moment you've pictured. You will not be wearing the good underwear. The matching bra and panties from Victoria's Secret with the snap crotch and the underwire yet lacy cups will be not on your body but back at home, either in the dirty laundry or tucked inside a drawer. Nor will you be wearing makeup, perfume, or perhaps even deodorant. Your hair will not be styled; you will be lucky if it is even washed. The Universe being the jokester It is, when you finally meet this seemingly perfect-for-you person, the first thought that will pop into your head will be, *Damn, I can look so much better than this!*

So goes my first meeting with Raj. It is a Sunday evening, September 2009. I am at Pop Burger in Manhattan's trendy Meatpacking District, doing something I have sworn never to do.

Speed dating.

In the eighties, love was a battlefield. In the (almost) 2010s, it is apparently a raceway.

Before today, I have never been speed dating. I say this with no small amount of pride. When I left my apartment that afternoon to meet my new friend, Nya, for a guided walking tour of the Lower East Side, I never imagined our outing would lead to…*this*.

Among Nya's plurality of part-time jobs—Martha Graham dancer, Gray Line tour guide, singer and actor—is speed-dating hostess. The latter is earlier revealed as we descend the steps of the Tenement Museum on Orchard Street, our fallback when the walking tour doesn't take off.

"Want to get a glass of wine somewhere?" I ask, loath to end the beautiful fall weekend by going home and doing laundry.

She shakes her head, looking regretful. "I wish I could, but I have to go to work."

"On a Sunday night?"

The question comes not from me but from Max, the winsome twenty-eight-year-old docent-cum-filmmaker who has followed us out. In the course of the forty-five-minute tour, he and I traded flirtatious badinage, lingering looks—and more than a few sparks.

Nya nods. "I'm hosting a speed-dating event tonight in Meatpacking." She divides her gaze between us, and a smile suffuses her face. "Hey, you two should come!"

Max and I exchange glances. "I don't think so," we say, almost in unison.

"C'mon," she coaxes. "I'm short two people. Admission's twenty dollars, but I'll comp you both."

Max's gaze veers back to me. "I'll go if you go."

"Deal." It won't really be speed dating if I have a pre-arranged date, or so I rationalize.

I reach the restaurant ten minutes before the "dating" is due to start. The bare-bones takeout storefront is deliberately deceptive. The event takes place in the clubby backroom. Walking inside, I note a long bar and more than a dozen white cloth-covered two-tops with numbered table tents.

Checking in the registrants, Nya hands me a sticker badge, a rating card, and a Sharpie. "Have fun," she says, her gaze going to the person in line behind me.

I stick on my name tag and head over to the bar. Other attendees mill about. Armed with a glass of chardonnay, I size up the scene. The men are friendly, the women not so much. Tricked out in slinky, strappy dresses and stilettos, they greet my bright hellos with curt nods and cautionary glances. With my jeans, scoop-neck T-shirt and boots, minimal makeup, and air-dried hair, no one can accuse me of trying too hard or even at all. For a brief moment, I wish I'd taken time to go home and change. Then again, I'm not here looking for love or even a date, speedy or otherwise. I have a date, or at least a dating prospect, en route. Until he arrives, I am a social ethnographer on par with Margaret Mead.

Raj and I meet *before* the speed dating starts. (He asks that I make that very clear.) The sea of our fellow registrants suddenly parts, and a cute young Indian man approaches.

"Hi, I'm Raj."

The first feature that strikes me is his eyes, velvety black-brown orbs exuding kindness, if a bit of uncertainty.

"Hope." I extend my hand, and he encloses it briefly in his.

The second thing I notice about him is his hair—wavy and thick, collar-length ebony shot with significant amounts of silver. *In his mid-thirties*, I think, and then remind myself to stop doing math and just have fun.

We slip into a conversation that feels surprisingly easy and, well, *real*. Raj tells me about his volunteerism with the city's Arts & Business Council and how moving it was to participate in reading the names of the fallen at the recent 9/11 Memorial. Ending the story, he asks, "How did you find out about tonight?"

I glance back to the check-in. "The event hostess is a friend. Actually, she's a friend-of-a friend. We hung out today, and she invited me here. Actually, she said she was short on people and needed bodies," I add, as though my being here is all about helping out Nya, as though I'm some kind of a *Sex and the City* Mother Teresa. "I've never done anything like this before. Actually, I'm not really doing this," I tack on, because it's suddenly really important that he not think I'm lame. Or a loser. "I'm a writer. I'm going to write a freelance article about the whole experience." I stop, realizing I'm rambling—and acting like an asshole.

Raj looks impressed. "You're a writer. That's cool."

I scan his face for signs he might be putting me on, but fortunately I find nothing but obvious sincerity. "I've never done this before either," he says. "A client told me about it. I almost didn't come." He hesitates. "Now I'm really glad I did." He smiles broadly, revealing an endearing glimpse of gum line.

By now, Max has arrived, but beyond a brief nod in his direction, I have as good as forgotten him. My sudden disinterest is apparently mutual. He takes up talking to a petite blonde in a spaghetti-strap dress, and we go our separate ways.

A recorded gong summons us to our places—quelle cheesy. Raj and I reluctantly part. "I'll see you later," he says.

"See you later," I answer, and head off to find my table.

There are thirty of us in all, equally divided between men and women. We settle in, the women at our tables, the men in line while Nya goes over the rules. Each date will last three minutes. When the gong sounds, the man must move on to the next table, no exceptions. There will be a mid-event break during which a snack will be served. Once everyone has met, the evening will end. Attendees go home where, from their—our—computers, they—we—can use the log-in and password printed on the rating card to go online and record their—our—selections. The service will notify each attendee of his/her matches, and then individuals are responsible for exchanging information and setting up an actual date. In other words, we are expected to be grown-ups.

Nya ends with, "Good luck, have fun," and then the gong goes off again.

The men file forward one at a time, sit at each table for three minutes, and make their pitches. "I express my creativity through…" has been pre-selected as the conversation icebreaker. We have been given rating cards to keep track of potential candidates for matches, but I leave mine lying on the seat. I don't make a love connection, but I do talk to several seemingly nice men. Everyone is perfectly polite. No one comes off as a loser.

Seven dates in, Nya announces the break. Trays of sliders are carried in. I scan the area for Raj, aka Cute Indian Guy, but he's nowhere in sight. Instead, one of my so far "dates," a handsome Japanese American with matching dimples, beats a path to my table and invites me to the bar for a glass of wine. I accept. We strike up a conversation, and I realize I'm having a pretty decent time.

The gong sounds, signaling the beginning of the second half of the session. I have eight more dates to go. Hopefully, one of them will be Raj.

My next guy up is mid-thirties, buzz cut, and a scary-bad dresser. His glittery T-shirt reveals thick tattooed forearms. He is carrying an actual clipboard and wearing a look that says he is approaching our "date" as serious business.

"I'm Jerry from Queens, and I express my creativity through sexual deviancy," he states, plunking down into the empty seat.

Wow, okay. I snatch my hand out of his bear paw and draw back. "I'm uh...Hope."

"I have twelve tattoos and multiple piercings," he announces with obvious pride. "Wanna know where they all are?"

Wow, again. I answer with an emphatic head shake. "Thanks, but I absolutely do not."

I'll pause here to say I totally get that I'm in New York City. It's not like I've never before encountered an alternative life-styler. Here, you don't have to venture much beyond your building entrance to encounter people engaged in sexual scenes so codified and specific they must rent storage space in New Jersey just to accommodate the gear. Still, this is Pop Burger in Meatpacking, not a fetish club in Alphabet City. And it is but six o'clock on a Sunday night. Shouldn't we at the very least... pace ourselves?

Jerry from Queens jerks his bullet-shaped head over to a numberless table set just outside our event periphery occupied by two women wearing heavy makeup, big hair, and skin-tight clothing. They meet my gaze and smirk.

"See those two over there? They're my slaves. I *own* them." He searches my face for a reaction. I guess I'm supposed to be really impressed or really freaked out or both.

Instead, I battle my twitching lips and choke back a chuckle. "Then why are you speed dating?"

The question draws a snort. He leans in closer, and I brace myself not to retreat. "Unlike these losers, *I* have an agenda." He gives the clipboard a purposive tap.

Small surprise, Jerry's agenda is to add a third "slave" to his merry ménage.

"Well, I have to tell you, Jerry, that person is so not me. I'm a straight arrow." I reach out to the rating card affixed to his clipboard. "In fact, you write 'straight arrow' right there next to my name."

I hadn't intentionally used a dominatrix voice, but Jerry from Queens cottons to my command with the docility of a pet poodle. He dutifully writes the words "straight arrow" beside my name, his silently moving lips keeping pace with the pencil.

The canned gong signals the end of our interlude. "Have a nice rest of the evening," I say, relieved for Jerry to haul himself up and away.

As soon as his back is turned, I grab my purse and dig inside for my travel-size bottle of hand sanitizer. "Thank God," I say aloud, finally finding it. I squeeze a generous dollop onto my palm and rub my hands briskly together. The feeling of being watched has me looking up. "Oh, I am so sorry."

Cute Indian Man—Raj—has quietly slipped into the cushioned booth seat across from me, so quietly I might have missed he was even there.

I extend a freshly sanitized hand. "I don't want to come off as a germaphobe, but you wouldn't believe the uh…conversation I had with that guy who just left."

Slim brown fingers wrap briefly about my palm, a firm but gentle grip. "That's okay," he says with a smile, giving me back my hand.

I share the interchange with Jerry from Queens, which suddenly strikes me as seriously funny. Shaking my head, I realize I'm laughing aloud—belly laughing—and that Raj is laughing with me.

"But I shouldn't be taking up our time talking about someone else," I say, contrite. Our three-minute "date" is sailing by—I sense it is almost up—and so far I have spent it recapping his predecessor.

He sends me a sympathetic look. "I'm just sorry you had to go through that."

I shrug, though his apparent compassion is refreshing—really refreshing. "When you're a writer, pretty much everything is material."

The glib words slip out before I can recall them. Once they do, I mentally kick myself. I like this guy, or at least I like what I've so far seen. The last thing I want is for him to think I'm mining him for "material."

"Actually, I'm thinking I may not write an article at all. I doubt the dating service would appreciate seeing my scenario with Jerry in print, and I wouldn't want to uh…cause any problems for Nya," I add, once again giving Mother Teresa stiff competition for that sainthood status.

The gong goes off again, for once far too soon. For the second time, we part with reluctance. I have six more dates to slug through. Thankfully, there are no more Jerrys. The evening ends slightly before nine o'clock. I expect people to hang out afterward, but the room clears as though a rat has been released.

Back home, I head over to my computer, log on to the dating site, and enter the IDs of my four possible matches: Max (for "old" time's sake), the Japanese-American guy with the crazily symmetrical dimples, and a handsome real estate agent who's admitted to recently ending a marriage. Saving the best for last, I put in Raj. My quick-beating heart tells me that my social ethnography research has stopped being "research" and morphed into something more, something...real. Drumming my nails on the computer cart, I wait. Less than a minute later, a message box flashes onto the screen. Raj and I are an instant match! A few minutes later, a short to-the-point e-mail lands in my in-box.

It was nice meeting you this evening. Are you free for dinner on Saturday?

Four years and many dinners later, we are happily together, cohabitating with cats and books and a bottomless hamper of dirty laundry. Underlying the age differences and the cultural differences are the differences-differences that demarcate any two people who not only come together as a couple but commit to remain that way. We are a classic case of opposites attracting—and our core values are the glue.

Among my faults is a tendency toward worrying. Okay, forget "tendency," my Anxiety Closet is pretty much the size of Versailles. When I'm in the throes of fretting, Raj will tease and even tickle me straight out of it. Sometimes, all it takes is for him to hoist his beautiful feathery black brows and cut me a look that so clearly says, *Really, Hope? Seriously!?!*

Writer though I am, I am fundamentally an extrovert, a social creature who fills her creative well from real-life interaction. I could be perfectly happy going out five nights a week. I *have* been perfectly happy going out five nights a week. In contrast, Raj is a homebody. One night out a week is all he needs, and strictly speaking he doesn't need that. Still, when we do go out, we have a great time. He doesn't need to socialize as much as I do, but that doesn't mean he isn't really good at it. He is.

Whereas a decent-weather day has me seizing on any excuse to be outside, he is happy to hibernate, surfing the Net or watching reruns of eighties sitcoms. No matter how brilliantly the sun is shining, no matter how dulcet the spring breeze or crisp the autumn air, he's content to stay indoors. On balance, winter has me feeling moody and restless, but he remains sunnily disposed across the seasons.

I'm a stickler for punctuality, while Raj is reliably an hour late for any non-work outing. If we are leaving town, his lateness comes closer to two hours, sometimes three. In lieu of starting out every road trip silently or not-so-silently seething, I have learned to bump up our official departure time by at least an hour. Imperfect, for sure, but it works.

And so do we. Raj and I work. We just do. Amidst all the differences, our mutual respect, our core compatibility, our *love* steers us to safe harbor time and time again.

Then again, we did lose our speed-dating virginity together. If that doesn't bond you, what will?

*Excerpted from *Forty Three is Too Old for a Fifth Floor Walkup: A Coming of Middle Age Memoir* © Hope Tarr

Hope Tarr earned a Master's Degree in Psychology and a Ph.D. in Education before coming to terms with the inconvenient truth: she didn't want to analyze or teach people. What she wanted was to write about them! Twenty-five romance novels later, Hope is doing just that, sharing her Happily Ever After stories with readers—and finding a few HEAs of her own. *Operation Cinderella*, the launch to her Suddenly Cinderella Series, has been optioned as a feature film by Twentieth Century Fox. Hope is also a cofounder and current curator of Lady Jane's Salon®, New York City's first and only monthly romance series now in its sixth year with seven satellites nationwide. She lives in Manhattan with her real-life romance hero and their rescue cats.

Visit her online at www.hopetarr.com, www.ladyjanesalonnyc.com, www.facebook.com/hopec.tarr, and www.twitter.com/hopetarr.

A Lost Friend, A Movie Star, A Man to Love Forever

Elf Ahearn

You might say it was a love triangle, but not in the technical sense. I was never torn between lovers. It's just that I met my husband and his best friend on July Fourth in 2002, and apparently, they were both attracted to me. That I married one and the other died has less to do with me than with what happens when a man's life stalls and he can't find a way to start it back up. At least that's how I think of it.

On that fabulous, fatal fourth, we were under the branches of a pine outside our hostess's clapboard home at Candlewood Lake in Connecticut, sitting on white plastic chairs and leaning our elbows on a rickety card table. Patrick, my future husband, sat next to me, and Peter, his best friend, stood at the grill cooking hotdogs. We were talking about our favorite musicians, and though we'd met only about a half hour ago, we were already joking and laughing. If puzzle pieces get happy when they fit, that's what we were feeling—puzzle pleased.

Patrick had an arm tossed over the back of his chair, and while he named folksingers, he looked at me in that searching way men have when they're seeking an invitation. They don't know that's what they're doing, but they let their eyes rove and rest, rove and rest on parts they like. Then they check back with your face to see if you're doing the same thing. But on that sunny afternoon, I gave the man no feedback. I was busy dating a psychopath and had just gone through a divorce, so I wasn't much interested in starting something new.

Then Patrick mentioned my favorite folksinger, Susan Werner, and I leaned a little closer. The card table creaked, and his deep, sexy voice got a hint more animated. He is six-foot-three. All that leg was sprawled out in front of him, and for the first time that day, I let my eyes rove and rest, though, as I said, my plate was full.

Peter chimed in that John Prine was his favorite folksinger. Back then, I didn't know who John Prine was, so the conversation switched to actors. Peter went inside for potato salad, while Patrick waxed poetic about Al Pacino versus Robert De Niro. And then he said Oscar-winning actress Ellen Burstyn was right up there with them. He wasn't trying to impress me, and he didn't come up with an actress just because I'm female and used to be in the theater—he actually started naming her films: *The Exorcist*, *Alice Doesn't Live Here Anymore*, *Resurrection*...

"I saw Ellen Burstyn in a movie that no one's ever heard of," I said, looking a little more closely at this big-boned Irishman with the gray-blue eyes. "The film was called *A Dream of Passion*, and she was brilliant."

To this day, I will never forget the expression in Patrick's eyes when I said the name of that movie. This doesn't sound romantic, but it was like a lizard snapping to attention—the twist of the body, the gaze that locks on. "I have a video of *A Dream of Passion*," he said.

At that moment, Peter slipped between us, dumping a bowl of potato salad on the table.

As dusk crept in and we waited for the fireworks over Candlewood Lake, I realized I had stumbled upon a gold mine of funny, intelligent men. Patrick, Peter and I talked and laughed about actors, movies, music and books. A citronella candle glowed in the center of the table, and we glowed back at it. Other partygoers sat down, ate their food and made a comment or two, but the bond was unbreakable. We weren't interested in talking to anyone else—only to each other.

The fireworks began at nine P.M. Just around the corner from our hostess's home was a causeway where we could sit and take in the show. By the time we walked there, it was crowded with onlookers. All the good places to sit, on the curb, or with your legs dangling under the guardrail, were taken. Patrick said he had folding chairs in his car, and I volunteered to help carry them back.

Peter jumped to his feet, dusted his backside and said, "I'll come, too." I could tell Patrick bristled a little at that, but like I said, I wasn't looking, so it didn't bother me.

More talking, more laughing. The three of us sat together in a row. Peter, me and Patrick, while the fireworks burst overhead, sometimes so near you'd swear the sparks would ignite us.

And then the display was over. We all said good night, and a drunken neighbor offered me fifty dollars to stay. He'd put on a show earlier throwing lit firecrackers for his German shepherd, who snapped and barked. The poor animal could have burned its tongue. Not a great way to end the evening, but I was really happy to have met these two awesome guys. We shook hands affectionately, and I gave Patrick a little tap on the back.

A year went by. Reports drifted in via a friend that I'd made quite the impression on the boys, but as I said, I had that psychopath, so I didn't pay much attention.

When summer returned, I heard our hostess planned to reprieve her party and that Peter and Patrick would be there. I was going to go, but at the last minute blew it off in favor of seeing my brother-in-law in a concert. The idea of meeting that drunken guy with the German shepherd didn't appeal to me. I felt guilty about not going, though, so I e-mailed the guys that I'd be happy to meet for breakfast.

Peter didn't write back, but Patrick did. He wasn't available for breakfast, but he said he'd like to take me to dinner. It's important to note that Patrick lived in New Jersey, about two hours away from my home in Connecticut.

On the night of our first official date, I pulled into the parking lot, and Patrick had his back to me. He was gazing at a decorative pond behind the restaurant, and when I called his name, he turned slowly and took off his sunglasses. I could tell he was trying for a James Bond cool. If he'd pulled it off, if he'd really been that debonair, I'd probably still be single, but how could I reject the sweetness of that goofy gesture? It meant he wanted to impress me—that he thought I was Bond Girl pretty.

We ate and talked. We talked so long, we closed the restaurant. Back out in the parking lot, I said something no guy had ever heard from me. "I'm not ready for this night to end." So we went to the neighborhood bar, and when they kicked us out, I still couldn't say goodbye. Chastely, I offered him my guest room.

A year later, Patrick and I were very much a couple. I threw a lot of parties in those days, and Peter always came early to help me prepare, to keep me laughing at his jokes and groaning at his puns. He'd lost his job—a communications business he'd started with a taller, more aggressive friend (Peter just topped five feet)—but they'd hired him back as a consultant. He had no girlfriend. His roommate's dog made him smile, especially the time it got so excited it peed on my shoe.

Fourth of July 2004, Patrick, Peter and I convened at our friend's home on Candlewood Lake. That year, Peter drove his brother's vintage Cadillac convertible. Blue with a white leather interior, it was the one thing he'd held on to after finding his brother dangling from a rope in the living room. A suicide note said, "I just couldn't hang on any longer."

On that night, we loaded into the back seat, and Peter gunned the engine. He spun around corners and sped down straightaways. I felt like a 1950s starlet with her hair blowing in the summer air. There was something reckless and young about being in the back of that car, though we were all out of our twenties.

When we got back to the party, Peter drank a lot and wanted to take us out for another spin. We said no and left soon after. He kept drinking, though, and then he got into that big car, zoomed down the road and got pulled over by the cops.

The next time we saw him, he was making good use of the bicycle Patrick once gave him as a present. He'd lost his license on a DWI, and then the dog who'd peed on my shoe died.

Christmas Day 2004, Patrick proposed. We were at my sister's house, and he'd bought me twelve presents. We sang "The Twelve Days of Christmas" as I opened each gift. The last line, traditionally "and a partridge in a pear tree," had been substituted with "and garbage with a flip lid." Yes, folks, he bought me a garbage pail.

Just before the "five golden rings" verse, Patrick stopped to make a phone call, which I thought was pretty annoying. When he hit the speaker button and my mother came on, however, he dropped to one knee and officially asked for my hand. (My father had passed in 1994.)

A long speech followed, and I don't remember a word of it. I was crying and laughing, and my sisters were all doing the same. Then Patrick took a dazzling ornament from the tree—a purple satin heart covered in gold braid and sequins—and from it he produced a golden ring. It was the ring his mother had worn—a simple plated band with worn places where another alloy shone through. "Five golden rings," we all sang at the top of our lungs.

Peter seemed genuinely happy for us when we told him, though we didn't see him for a while.

In late June 2005, I got a call at work from Peter asking if I wanted to see folksinger John Prine at Town Hall in New York City. Patrick would meet us at the venue.

On the way down, Peter talked about the Newport Film Festival, how he'd gone with nothing more than a ticket in his hand but became a vital volunteer. They'd made him a bouncer. For a small man, that must have been the ego trip of a lifetime. He'd shaved his head, talked tough and rested a hand on my thigh, which pissed me off.

We stopped at a coffee shop and bought sandwiches for dinner. I picked roast beef, but it had gone bad. Peter promised to pull off the highway so I could pick up a slice of pizza or something, but he kept driving. In the city we ended up at an expensive restaurant, forgoing the opening act so I could eat. Now he was mad at me.

The concert was amazing, but the ride home was sullen.

That September, I rented out my house in Connecticut, quit my job and moved into a new home in New York State with Patrick. As we were setting up housekeeping, we heard occasionally from Peter that he'd become involved in a film festival in his hometown of Bethel, Connecticut. He promised to let us know when it happened, but we never got an invitation.

Then the woman with the house on Candlewood Lake called the morning of December 2, 2005. The night before, she said, her voice cracking with emotion, Peter had lain down on the tracks and waited for the eight-thirty commuter out of New York. When I told Patrick, he hit the top of the bathroom vanity, screaming, "No! No! No!"

As we prepared for our wedding, Patrick and I told Ellen Burstyn, who'd agreed to officiate, all about Peter. She promised to mention him in the ceremony—to say how strange it was not to have him there—because we'd been a trio. We'd been three friends who loved each other enough that Peter should have known he'd have a permanent place in our lives.

Before we exchanged rings, Susan Werner, whom Patrick hired as a surprise wedding gift to me, sang a song I wish Peter could have heard. It's called "Attend the Sky," and the first verse says:

> Have you ever had life pour in like sunlight through the window
> Have you ever had love pour down like summer in the rain
> Have you ever had justice come and settle in your corner
> Well if you never have
> It will happen one day.

Elf Ahearn—yes, that is her real name—writes Regency romances "with a Gothic twist." Having been an actress, she can't resist ladling such high-tension drama into her novels that she feels compelled to warn of her Gothic tendencies. Her books, *A Rogue in Sheep's Clothing* and *Lord Monroe's Dark Tower,* are available at Amazon.com, Barnes & Noble and all the other online spots where reading material lurks. She is blissfully married to Patrick Ahearn, with whom she shares a pesky (yet adorable) cat named Sufie.

Visit Elf online at www.elfahearn.com.

Acceptance

LEANNA RENEE HIEBER

I grew up in rural Ohio inventing ghost stories, was involved in any piece of theater or art I could have my hand in, started my first novel around the age of twelve (a sequel to *The Phantom of the Opera* because I didn't like the ending), starred in multiple high school and regional youth productions, got my BFA in theater performance and graduated with a lot of drama under my belt.

And in my personal life.

Not only have I always been a dynamo of unwieldy energy, but it took a long time and a lot of tumult before I understood the concept of leaving my work at work. My love life was just as unpredictable and often unstable as my on-stage lives as I toured the regional theater circuit in different professional shows. But a girl can only take so much drama in every sphere for so long. My path needed a fresh perspective, in art and in life. I needed to be grounded, and I needed to make a brave, bold change.

So, with about two weeks' notice, I packed up my Ford Taurus and drove to New York City, where I knew only my future roommate and one other soul.

I knew I would sort myself out in a city that would sort me. Creatively and emotionally, I was at an impasse. A big move to *the* enormous, daunting metropolis would force me to leave serially unhealthy relationships and finally live for myself and my dreams. I also hoped New York would help me determine which of my great loves would be my true calling: the stage or the page.

I worked random miserable jobs and went to innumerable miserable auditions, hoping I wasn't delusional in thinking I was working toward something. My first year in the city, I occasionally dated, but I'm awkward. I was certainly *not* living *Sex and the City*. I hated the initial dating process as much as I still hate that show. I made friends and focused on myself. And, as a progressive left-wing Christian who always believed my artistic passions were a heavenly calling, I wondered what God had in store for me.

Torn between actress and author, I wondered if I had to pick a side. I went to a Broadway callback and all I could think about was my book. I shifted gears. I stopped auditioning. I started querying the novel I'd begun writing while an intern at the Cincinnati Shakespeare Company a few years prior.

I got a job as a tour guide on the big red double-decker buses in the city, hoping that would suit me better than working the frontlines at Starbucks Times Square and at a law firm, the latter a particularly ill fit.

As a lifelong Goth girl (no, it's not a phase), wearing a white polo and khakis to work at the tour bus company was *hardly* my idea of style (the horror!). I certainly wasn't looking for a date when I befriended the outgoing, exuberant Marcos, a fellow tour guide who said that overhearing me discuss my prayerful quest toward artistic discernment had piqued his interest. And he thought I was hot.

We were both vegetarians, liberal, Protestant Christians with Lutheranism and Methodism in our backgrounds. He was a dancer and musician. We were artists to the core of our beings. We had in common all the great things friendships are made of. I was not looking for a relationship. Not even dating. No.

He'd seen me only in a white polo shirt, for the love of God. My inner Gothling was withering day by sunny khaki-clad day.... We hung out for a period of time after work. We would wave to each other from one tour bus to another. He sang me his songs. I told him about my books. We went to see a movie. We kissed. We fell into a relationship before we really knew what hit us.

But before I could really let myself go, I had one task for him.

I handed him the manuscript of what would become my debut novel, *The Strangely Beautiful Tale of Miss Percy Parker*, a Gothic Victorian saga about a group of ghost-busters in 1888 London at the time of Jack the Ripper, filled with sweeping drama, intense action and romance, underpinned by Greek mythology.

I handed him the tome and said, "If you want to really understand me, read this."

Understanding me as an artist was the key to my heart.

And he did.

If he hadn't accepted this early task, I'd have bailed. I needed my career and my passion to be as much a driving force in my life as my relationships were. The two didn't have to be at cross-purposes.

Even though Marcos wasn't a big fiction reader, he took this on with as much enthusiasm as he had our early adventures. And because his earnest interest made me feel safe, I allowed myself to fall.

He fit my type: tall, dark and handsome; enthusiastic; personable; clever; and talented. The difference from my previous relationships was that he was stable, responsible, and unfailingly into me. That was new for me, that kind of confidence. We laughed at each other's jokes and shared the same nerdy love for various sci-fi/fantasy fandoms. And our shared faith was something both of us had found severely lacking in past relationships. He seemed as interested in growth as a person and as an artist as I was. The foundations were strong.

There were bumps, as there are in any relationship, but we rode them out, realizing we wanted this to work more than we didn't. I tried, and am still trying, to learn Spanish out of respect for his Puerto Rican heritage. I try to understand him as much as he has tried to understand me.

One early instance of his effort at understanding remains one of my favorite things anyone has done for me, something that crystalizes who he is and what we have.

During the first couple of years of our relationship, I had yet to get an agent or any nibble on my novel. I faced countless rejection letters as any aspiring author does, and I was feeling disheartened. One day I came home to find something on my bed in a FedEx envelope. It was an acceptance letter.

From God.

Marcos had written out, very Hogwarts-style (I'm *obsessed* with Harry Potter and very active in the fandom along with my best friends and family; Marcos had to accept this early on, too), an acceptance letter of my gifts, my talents, my pursuits, and my purpose. And he had it "sent" from what we both believe to be the highest authority and resource in the world: the Holy Spirit.

My partner had found a brilliantly, thoughtfully clever way to not only tell me he was on my side, but that he supported me on every level—emotionally, spiritually and literally. He knew how hard I was working, how disheartened I was at the whole long process, so a little clever letter was a big, delightful deal.

It was not long after his heavenly acceptance letter that I gained an agent. Not long after that that I gained a contract. We moved in together. I published more books. My internal war over which of my art would take precedence—my books—was won, and so was my heart.

Years later, on our seventh anniversary, he would propose at my favorite spot in Central Park. He did a perfect job. (Well, I'd written a sort of guidebook in having one of my characters propose in that same spot, only my character botched it. Marcos, as always, paid attention.) He played me a proposal song he wrote for our anniversary, went down on one knee at the beautiful Bethesda Terrace during the proposal verse, and presented the most unique and exquisite cameo dating to 1875, a ring for which he'd searched several states over, having listened to my request for a non-traditional, conflict-free ring that was a piece of my beloved late 19th century. He said the figure in the cameo reminded him of Miss Percy Parker, heroine of that debut series he had accepted on behalf of God years prior.

Not only had he kept reading me through the years, but he'd acted upon his knowledge. What a good student of me he had become. (I hope to earn the same passing grades.)

At the time of writing this piece, Marcos and I are recently married, our bilingual ceremony presided over by his ninety-eight-year-old Puerto Rican grandmother, the first island-born woman to be ordained in the Lutheran church. She is a brilliant, headstrong woman, quite a character, quite a role model. Marcos celebrates in me that same feisty, fierce and intelligent independence he's seen in the powerful women in his life.

A good partner requires a good partnership. We're a work in progress. I'm still trying to learn Spanish. He owns more black clothing than he used to, and we trade off going to dance salsa and to a Goth club. I dress him up as the hero of my Strangely Beautiful saga—he's such a good sport and looks so fetching in a frock coat—and I attend his musical and dance performances as a supportive audience member.

Our purposes and our callings have been affirmed by each other and by our spirituality. We're an ongoing acceptance letter to one another.

Leanna Renee Hieber is an actress, playwright, and the award-winning, nationally bestselling author of Gothic Victorian fantasy novels with romantic elements, such as the Strangely Beautiful saga, the Magic Most Foul saga and the forthcoming Eterna Files from Tor/Macmillan. Her acclaimed Strangely Beau-tiful saga will re-issue in new editions from Tor/Macmillan in 2014. A lifelong Goth girl, she lives in New York City with her husband and their beloved rescued lab rabbit. She owns more corsets than is reasonable, channels Narcissa Malfoy at various conventions, loves hearing a good ghost story or creating one on the spot, and can be found in full Victorian regalia (in various shades of black) at all public appearances. A proud member of performers unions Actors Equity and SAG-AFTRA, she works in film and television on shows like Boardwalk Empire.

For more, please visit her at www.leannareneehieber.com, follow her on Twitter @leannarenee, and like her on Facebook at facebook.com/lrhieber.

Unexpected Treasures[*]

Lisa Renée Jones

I believe your true love should be your best friend, and I'm writing about mine from my honeymoon hotel. I found my true love in a Barnes & Noble in Austin, Texas. I had a cozy seat there that I loved for writing. It was my escape and my place to get lost in my stories. I'd write awhile, order a white mocha, and then take a break to go stroll the romance section of the store. Diego, my husband as of yesterday (November 9), used to go to Barnes & Noble to study for his MCAT for medical school and to get lost in the books he, too, loves.

One night we were both there, and being the gym rat that I am, he recognized me from the gym. He came up to me, and we started talking. After that, we ran into each other often at Barnes & Noble, and soon we were friends, but the kind that makes you tingle all over. The best kind! During one of those talks, I remember him asking my age. He dodged the question when I wanted to know his, though I didn't realize he had until later. Weeks after that conversation, after our bond had really grown, I learned that he was nine years younger than I am and that he had held back that fact because he just knew it was going to freak me out. It did! But it was too late when I found out. I'd already fallen hard.

One thing I love about Diego is that he is a smell-the-roses kind of person. I remember walking along a sidewalk with him early on in our romance when he spotted a chocolate store. He grabbed me and pulled me across the street toward the store and was so excited to go inside and experience it with me. I remember wondering when I'd ever been SO excited about something as small as visiting a chocolate store ever in my life, and yet I was in that moment. I knew I was in love that day. He made me stop and enjoy the moment, and he has done that over and over so many times since I met him. And I need that, as I'm truly a workaholic. Diego and I have these little things we do together that have become special to me and my way of relaxing. I think the little things were really missing from my life before I met him.

Another special part of our relationship is our shared belief that taking actions to achieve your dreams means happiness in life. His support of my dreams has been unbelievable and touching. When he met me, my writing career barely had legs. I'd left the corporate world to be a starving artist, and he supported that decision in a way most of the people in my life didn't. He truly believed in me, even at times when I did not. Sometimes, I wonder how he did and how he knew it was all going to be worth the fight.

The story behind the Inside Out series is a fun part of how Diego is invested in my dreams and how his belief in me and my writing led to me finally establishing myself as a writer. We had limited funds to pay the bills, as my writing wasn't paying much, and my fiancé was working at a physical therapy clinic that closed down suddenly. I'd read an article on buying and selling storage units and I thought…hmm. Of course, we had little cash to invest and everything to lose, but Diego was intrigued and wanted to check out the next auction posted. Back then there was no amazing online resource like Storage Treasures. We had to dig in public postings and call around to storage facilities to find out what was happening when.

So, knowing virtually nothing about what he was doing, Diego took off to his first auction with the understanding he would spend no more than three hundred dollars. Back then, auctions were not competitive because they weren't very well publicized. I proceeded to work on a book and wait. The next thing I know, he's telling me he spent eight hundred dollars. "But don't worry! It's worth at least three thousand." I was freaking out. We had rent to pay. Let me tell you, the romance almost ended there! I was really freaking out when our tiny apartment was suddenly filled with furniture and boxes and I couldn't even move around in it. The unit ended up doing well for us, so I decided I'd keep him.

Several years later, we were heavily into auction hunting, and I was still a struggling writer. After purchasing several units, Diego got the flu and was in bed sick. He'd stumbled onto a journal in one of the new boxes, and I have no idea what possessed him to do it, but he grabbed it and took it to bed with him. From there it was pretty funny. He'd sit up suddenly and say, "Someone died next door and the police are there!" Then later, "Oh my God, she's pregnant again." We did a lot of laughing over that journal, and Diego decided I *had* to write a story about a storage unit with a mystery. "Do that sexy thing you do, but someone has to die!"

At the time, I was very busy with books I owed to publishers and didn't have time to write the story he kept pressing me to write, but that didn't discourage him. He kept at me about it, and the idea churned in my mind. He just knew in his bones this idea was going to be magic for me. Finally, I was done with the contracts I had in place, and I knew deep down on some level Diego was right about this premise. I needed to write the story about the journal. I'd developed an idea and characters who were begging to be brought to life. So I started writing, and when I was done, I knew this series was the best I'd ever been as a writer, and I hoped readers would feel the same way. Fortunately, not only did readers respond well, but my agent loved it, and so did a cable network and Suzanne Todd (producer of *Memento*, *Alice in Wonderland*, *Austin Powers*, and more), who is now developing the television series.

It's amazing to me how that decision to go to that first auction changed our lives, but even more so how the man in my life inspired me to write the series that changed our lives. It's truly a joy for me to have him by my side to celebrate the way it turned out, but not because of the success. What makes this special to me is that he was there when I was ready to quit, and when I cried and doubted, he *never* doubted. He was my strength when I didn't have it. He was a friend when I wasn't one to myself.

And finally we got married. Some people have asked why it took us years to get married. The answer is that we'd both been married before and we knew we loved each other. We didn't want to do it in the middle of a struggle. We wanted to do it in a moment that felt like a real celebration of our life together. That's exactly what our wedding was, too. It was a wonderful chance for us to look at where we have been and what we have built *together* and to celebrate it as man and wife and best friends.

*Previously published in Love Letter Magazine.
Reprinted with permission of the author.

New York Times and *USA Today* bestselling author Lisa Renée Jones is the author of the highly acclaimed *Inside Out* Trilogy, which has sold to more than ten countries for translation with negotiations in process for more, and has now been optioned by STARZ Network for a cable television show to be produced by Suzanne Todd (*Alice in Wonderland*). Since beginning her publishing career in 2007, Lisa has published more than thirty books with publishers such as Simon and Schuster, Avon, Kensington, Harlequin, NAL, Berkley and Ellora's Cave, as well as crafting a successful indie career. Prior to publishing, Lisa owned a multistate staffing agency that was recognized many times by the *Austin Business Journal* and also praised by *Dallas Women Magazine*. In 1998 LRJ was listed as the #7 growing women-owned business in *Entrepreneur* magazine. Lisa loves to hear from her readers.

You can reach her at www.lisareneejones.com, and she is active daily on Twitter and Facebook.

PART II

How We Wed

A "Killer" Wedding

J. Kenner

I very rarely write epic romance. On the contrary, in most of my forty-plus books, the hero and the heroine get together, fall in love, and win their happily-ever-after in a span of months, sometimes even weeks. Why do I lean that way? Because, to me, whirlwind is reality.

I met my husband in January of 1993, and we were married in October of that same year. Although, when you factor in my deep, dark secret—I don't actually remember meeting him that January—our courtship was much, much shorter.

It all happened because of football. More specifically, because I don't watch it. (Seriously, I'm doing well knowing that the Super Bowl is a football game and not a very large culinary dispensing device.)

But back in 1993, I was living in Los Angeles and working as an attorney. I'd used my 1992 Christmas bonus to buy a Fabulous Couch. You know—the kind of furniture that requires capital letters. And this one was truly Fabulous. Deep enough to double as a twin-size guest bed if you took off the back cushions. Overstuffed with goose down. Designed in a shabby chic style. And white. Very, very white. And I was desperate to keep it that way.

When Super Bowl day came, my BFF from high school, Steve, asked if he could borrow my apartment to have some friends over to watch the game. He actually lived next door, but his roommate (another high school friend from Texas) had non-football-related plans. Plus, they didn't have a television in the living room—only in their separate bedrooms, and that really wasn't the Super Bowl vibe he was going for.

Since I was going to happily shop in the mostly empty stores that day, I agreed—then left to explore IKEA while he hosted a gathering. But, of course, I had to first strictly warn him not to get my new couch dirty.

I came home hours later, the proud owner of a humongous as-is dining room table from the chip-and-dent section of IKEA. The guys in my apartment helped out—all except one who, I learned later, had injured his back not long before. The guy, Don, who I would later marry.

From his perspective, he thought he was watching the game at Steve's apartment and wondered why my friend was so incredibly paranoid about getting pizza sauce on the couch. "It was a great couch, but the fastidiousness didn't seem Steve-like," he told me later. He was right, of course. After the Northridge quake, we were all hard-pressed to say whether Steve's then-non-roommate-shared apartment had actually been shaken up, because it really didn't look much different than normal. Steve, I am assuming, is not reading this essay. Let's keep it that way, shall we? At any rate, Don-the-husband-to-be offered to guard the couch while the rest of the guys schlepped my table up from the car to my apartment. Who says chivalry is dead?

So much for the cute meet, huh?

Fast-forward to summer. *Jurassic Park* is opening, and Steve and two of his friends from work are coming along, Richard and Richard's roommate, Don. I join them, and Don and I hit it off. It's nice. We share popcorn. I am blissfully unaware that he didn't help move my table, or that he was ever in my apartment, much less that he had spent hours leaning against my couch drinking beer and watching football.

Movie, then Ben & Jerry's ice cream, all lovely and sweet and sweaty-palm-inducing. Especially since we'd shared a tub of popcorn and the inevitable hand brush. And far too quick to come to a tame and friendly close. But there were vibes. I was sure there were vibes.

Since I'd already planned a July Fourth party at my apartment complex's pool, the next weekend I wandered down to the Ventura Boulevard Book Star, where these three guys worked, and casually asked Don if he'd like to come, too. Richard was coming, after all; they could come together.

They did, and thanks in part to the power of my amazing margaritas, Don and I hit it off even more. While most of my guests stayed outside by the pool, we were inside near the kitchen having Deep, Meaningful Conversations over many, many margaritas.

We talked about everything from friends to books to music to movies. We learned that we both went to the same undergraduate school and that we were both from Texas and had moved to Los Angeles to seek our fortunes. He learned that I'd never seen a Hong Kong film.

And so we set a date. The next Friday, we went to see John Woo's *The Killer* (awesome movie) at a wonderful theater in Santa Monica. If you're not familiar with the story, the hero is a paid assassin. In the course of a job, he accidentally blinds a singer, who he then takes care of. Naturally, she gets caught in the midst of a mess.

There's a beautiful song near the beginning of the movie that she sings (she was played by a well-known Hong Kong singer). And the soundtrack is just amazing.

I say all that not just to set the stage, but as foreshadowing. (And, now, hopefully, you're wondering what it is that I'm foreshadowing!)

But I'm getting ahead of myself.

After the movie, we did the typical LA date stuff. Walked on the Third Street Promenade. Window-shopped. Had dinner at a sadly horrible Indian food restaurant. (But it does make a good story to laugh about now.) My friend Steve called me Sunday night to ask how the date went. My answer? "It's still going."

Yeah, you could say we hit it off.

A few weeks later we decided to take off for a weekend in Vegas. Later, Don told me he'd thought about asking me to marry him that weekend but decided it was too soon. Instead, he waited until July—the day before I went home to Austin for my high school reunion!

We ended up getting married in Texas in October that year—ten months after we met, but only four months after we *really* met.

The ceremony was small—and here's the part that I foreshadowed: We wanted it to be truly ours. More than that, we wanted it to represent our growing love of Hong Kong action films, especially *The Killer*, which we'd watched on our first date. (It doesn't sound romantic, I know, but the song is truly beautiful.)

Now, this was in the days before iTunes and MP3s and easy access to everything in the world over the Internet and with Google. For that matter, to get most of the movies that we wanted to watch, we had to drive across Los Angeles and poke around in Chinatown. We did that for entertainment…and then later we did it to find *The Killer*, because we wanted to rip the music and use it in our wedding.

We managed to find three different versions, both with different translations of the song we loved. Two were happy and romantic. One was more or less a funeral dirge. We pretended the third translation didn't exist.

We hired a friend who was good with tape manipulation to pull the soundtrack for us. It wasn't perfect, but we figured it would work.

Then we saw that the laser disc Criterion edition of *The Killer* was being released—and that John Woo himself would be signing at Virgin Records on Sunset. (I told you, this was the Dark Ages.)

Off we went. We were on a wedding mission. Determined to get a wedding present to each other and to ask John Woo if a soundtrack for the movie existed in any way, shape, or form. (As far as we could tell, no such creature existed.)

We went. We stood in line. We gaped at Mr. Woo, who is an incredibly nice man. He signed our laser disc set, and we told him that the movie was our first date, that we were using the song in our wedding, and we were having trouble finding that soundtrack. He informed us that soundtracks to movies aren't as common in Hong Kong as they are here. (That may have changed since then; I don't know.)

He asked for our address and we gave it...and a few weeks later we received studio-quality cassette tapes with the movie's music! (Not only that, but for many years after we received holiday cards from Mr. Woo. How cool is that?)

So we were able to use the music from *The Killer* in our wedding, much to the mortification of my grandmother, who had expected the bridal march, even though I had warned her ahead of time.

The wedding was small, wonderful, and utterly us. And, really, what more can you ask of a wedding?

So when people ask me if I think that a whirlwind romance is realistic, I have to answer yes. After all, twenty years and two kids later, mine is still going strong!

J. Kenner (aka Julie Kenner and J.K. Beck) is the *New York Times*, *USA Today*, *Publishers Weekly*, and *Wall Street Journal* bestselling author of more than forty novels, novellas and short stories in a variety of genres. Praised by Publishers Weekly as an author with a "flair for dialogue and eccentric characterizations," J.K. writes a range of stories including super sexy romances, paranormal romance, chick lit suspense and paranormal mommy lit.

Visit her website at www.juliekenner.com.

Wedding 101 for the Anti-Bridezilla

Patience Bloom

I'm not sure this is happening. Did I wake up in a dream? A charming, handsome man is sitting across from me in my favorite Mexican restaurant. We're eating chips and salsa. Somehow, my date has helped me tolerate dining out again—a miracle for a hermit girl like me. The sun is blazing hard, making the seats sticky, and I regret wearing my ill-fitting khaki skirt rather than an airy sundress. The city heat usually irritates me, though not so much now. This night is different, certainly no ordinary Thursday evening.

I take in every detail, since people will ask about our story. In my mental log, I note the June humidity; Sam's sports jacket, which covers up his shirt drenched from nervousness; the frozen margarita he just ordered to combat those nerves; the relatively empty restaurant since we're on my geriatric schedule.

I sip my Sprite because my mouth is dry, though I mostly need something to do with my hands, and pretend to be oblivious of Sam Bloom's imminent marriage proposal. We girls often smell these things from miles away, so I'm able to remain calm while he puts a beautiful ring on my finger, and asks *that* question. You know the one.

"Of course, I'll marry you," I answer.

There is no squealing, no bended knee, shaking, or the hand to mouth with me crying over the opening of the box. A violinist doesn't serenade us, nor does my entire family or roster of friends materialize to congratulate us. No one around us sees our engagement. In fact, this wedding proposal is casual, sedate, intimate—like an everyday occurrence in our brief courtship.

As I stare at him, I'm a little stunned. How did this happen? A year ago, I had given up on dating, didn't even want a boyfriend. Romance was too much trouble, and I liked my own company much more. Sam changed the order of things with one Facebook friend request. Ten months later, I'm madly in love with him and about to get married. The universe has a way of surprising you. Between you and me, though, I am happy just to have him in my life. We could live in sin forever and that would be fine with me.

Oh, who am I kidding? I love this new rock on my finger!

A few minutes after Sam Bloom proposes to me, my new bridal situation demands my immediate attention. Instead of glorying in our love, I let Sam temporarily fall off my radar as long-dormant girly thoughts take control of my mental synapses: sparkly bride earrings, bridal hair, beautiful bridal dress, a day where everyone says how beautiful I look, signing everything as Mrs. Bloom, that "smug married" smile. Even more superficialities race through my brain, such as:

- White is not my color. Forget ivory, too. That's like a consolation color when you don't look great in white.
- And yet, I love the idea of a veil—especially since it might hide my crow's-feet. Maybe a nice white veil could be worn at all times! It'll be my thing.
- Will I be a bridezilla? Just once, it might be fun to scream my rage while immersed in tulle and, please, let it be filmed.
- Can I do the wedding-cake tasting now?

- Since I've never read a bridal magazine, what's proper for an over-the-hill bride? What in marshmallow-fluff-mermaid-ruching hell do I do?

It's like my life flashing before my eyes, though for a delightful cause. Oh, the possibilities! Me, *me...I* am going to be a *bride*!

As I look down at the ring once again, I feel a strange excitement, an urgent need to start right away. Forget the rest of dinner, I'm getting married. Since I'm not so good with crowds, Sam and I will have a quiet wedding down at City Hall, like next week. Or I could sacrifice my people-phobia for a gigantic, themed wedding with everyone—togas, circus performers, mead. Perhaps I'll pull a Julia Roberts and invite people to a party that turns into a wedding. Whatever happens, this is a joyous event.

While Sam wolfs down his burrito and eats most of mine, more rose-colored wedding visions dance in my head. Beaded bodices. Jordan almonds. A long train behind me. Flower girls making everyone laugh. An elegant hairstyle. Putting simple gold bands on our fingers. Dancing to eighties music. More cake. I'll smile through it all. And I won't faint like on those YouTube videos. No insanity whatsoever when I get married.

Sam and I fit so well together. We can't help but have harmonious nuptials. At home, he cooks, I eat, and then he does the dishes. He checks up on me during the day, just to say hello. I make the bed, he messes it up at least three times for his nap, post-nap nap, and sleeping at night. After he hauls down the laundry, I iron and starch his shirts. We even go to the gym together, wave and smile at each from across the room—me on my treadmill, him on his stair-climber. It's practically a *Hart to Hart* affair. Now our felicity is about to be written in stone. I get to do this for the rest of my life. There's a deep peace over this new journey, but also, it's wildly uncharted territory for me.

So, once Sam and I walk home, tell our relatives and change our Facebook statuses to "Engaged," I do what I do best: make lists and break down the new project. The very first lesson I need to learn is:

Try not to drive the groom so crazy that he bails. Getting married might turn me into a Tasmanian devil of insecurity beforehand. And because of my job as an editor of romance novels, I know all about the jilted-at-the-altar situation. The sweet bride has put blood, sweat and tears into her relationship, but the fiancé never shows up. If that isn't enough, *Four Weddings and a Funeral* is a graduate course in how not to get married. Sam proposed to a moderately sane woman. I vow to stay calm, striking out on my own in my Wedding 101 education. Several truths become clear straight off:

Weddings cost a bajillion dollars. Oh, the sticker shock. It takes a lot of work to put on a wedding, even a small one—and a whole lot of Benjamins. Forget about putting your children through college. Or buying a house. If you want a wedding, be prepared to fork it over. You can cry over your glass of tap water, because that's all you can afford.

If you're of a certain age, stop referring to yourself as an over-the-hill bride: At forty-two, I wonder why I even need to have a wedding. We have no kids. My family doesn't care if I live with my boyfriend—oops, *fiancé*. Do I want people to come witness this very personal ritual? Sure, I do, because it's fun. No one cares about my age, so I shouldn't. Gloria Steinem first married at sixty-six. Everyone deserves a party, a wedding, if they want one. I deserve an amazing partner. The minute I stop questioning my worthiness, a part of me relaxes. Until I look over at Sam, who's doing very little to help me plan this shindig.

Don't expect anyone to work harder on the wedding than you. Since we (I) decide to marry within six months, the venue, dress and invites need to be done like yesterday. And the minute Sam puts the ring on my finger he seems to think his job is done. Does he not love me? Plus, getting him to agree on the wedding date was just too easy.

In that restaurant, on that special June day, I asked him, "So, when do you want to get married?"

"How about in a year?" he answered.

"How about next February?" I said.

"Sure."

And by February, I meant January, as in over a long weekend. See? My decision. Wedding planning is kind of all about the bride. Or if you've watched *My Big Fat Greek Wedding*, the bride's family. I'm working awfully hard for this ring, but no one else is. When I complain to Sam about his lack of involvement, he says he doesn't want to "step on anyone's toes." Translation: This is not my thing, but I'll show up. Throughout the planning, I'm told this is normal. He cooks and does my laundry, so I'm okay with his adhering to this one gender stereotype. His stellar presence more than makes up for it.

Remember to put yourself into the wedding. To mask my fear of the public eye and my ignorance of wedding regalia, I think a quickie City Hall service is the way to go. Or a small twenty-person wedding in a tiny room, followed by a reception in a bigger room with more guests. But Sam, my mother and everyone else want an actual wedding—the whole enchilada. Big wedding it is.

After several sessions of breathing into a paper bag, I send out an SOS to my married friends and coworkers. I know nothing about any of this wedding stuff. A romance author sends me three wedding-planning books. Another suggests joining The Knot. My colleagues send me dress ideas. And invitations? Must be on thick paper (preferably cream) with lovely embossed lettering. I have fantasies of being Martha Stewart and doing the invites myself. With great ambition, I run to my stationery store and buy multicolored paper, inks, stickers and rubber stamps. For days, I sit in the middle of glitter mayhem, then share the results with my brother.

"Um, this isn't a kindergarten class, Patience. You need real invitations," my brother says, trying not to laugh. Which means a bajillion dollars more.

I flex new muscles, noticing that much of my wedding is about pleasing groups of people—the vegetarians, the non-glutens, the lactose intolerant, various religious factions, those who "hate that loud rock music," the allergic, the children, and the ones who might get falling-down drunk by cake-cutting time. It's a pleasure to accommodate their needs, but I also crave one element that says, "This is a Patience wedding!" So I claim Duran Duran's "Rio" as my walking-down-the-aisle song. I'm set now.

When picking out your dress, think about Aunt Mary Anne and not how you want to be a Las Vegas showgirl. Of course, your dress can be a duck costume or a respectable champagne pantsuit. Because of my age, guests might rather see me in that pantsuit. The problem is that I already wear pantsuits to work and conferences. My bridal dress should be special, once in a lifetime. Like, what about some feathers covering my legs, tassels, and a massive Cher headdress? When will I ever get another chance like this? I compromise with a blue gown—slightly showy, hides sins, and my aunt won't be mortified. Sam takes about two minutes choosing a black suit and crisp white shirt. Grooms have it so easy, it's sickening. But still, done!

Make peace with the fact that something will go wrong. Perfection doesn't exist. A huge whopper of a nightmare could rain down on your wedding day. Then again, I try not to let this become a self-fulfilling prophecy. The more you obsess about spewing at the altar, the more breakfast could return for an encore. As I frantically search for the perfect dress, the perfect wedding-party gifts, the perfect seating chart, the idea of one wrong move renders me catatonic with nervousness. I plan for every wedding nightmare: snowstorm, no officiant, groom imploding minutes before, food poisoning over the spinach cream thing I'm not quite sure about, tripping on my heels, mascara running down my face, and everyone having a rotten time.

Then again, what about all that goes right?

What about the fact that my relationship is a deeply fulfilling one and nothing needs to be perfect? The wedding could be a bore, but we'll still be happy. Thanks to the great mystery of life, I never prepare for what actually does go wrong (it came in threes for me). But given how lucky I feel with Sam, I take these imperfections in stride. A bride should be determined to have fun, no matter what.

Wedding guests will have a good time as long as there's food (and booze). Really, no one cares that much about the Jordan almonds or if you have his/hers coasters. Two weeks before the big day, I can't quite make up my mind about this one....

"Mom, shouldn't we have wedding favors? Like Sam and Patience M&M's?" I ask my mother, who must know I have ulterior motives. Just think of how many bags we'll have left over—bags I can stash in my secret chocolate drawer.

"That's ridiculous," Mom says. Of course it is, just one more expense on what is already costing a bajillion dollars.

Besides, it's a little thing. My wedding won't hinge upon whether or not we have his/hers M&M's. For guests, weddings are mostly funfests. You get to dress up, eat food, see loved ones, and dance. Why worry about the details?

Soak up every moment of your wedding. If I spend my day being hysterical, I will miss the joy of marrying Sam. By some miracle, I love every second of my wedding day.

Even three years later, I can go through the entire day and feel the same giddiness. I remember waking up, knowing I would become his wife; the beauty team that made me into a bride; Sam's loud voice saying his vows, how his green eyes seemed bigger than ever; his cute haircut and the yellow rose in his lapel; seeing both sides of my family interact after thirty years of no contact; our first dance to "My Eyes Adored You"; the torture of seeing the food but not getting to taste any of it until the reception was over; and, most of all, the bliss of becoming Sam's wife.

The truth is that I didn't need to marry Sam to feel happy or loved, but it was pretty great icing. Falling in love with such a special man was the real cake.

Patience Bloom is the author of *Romance Is My Day Job* (Dutton, February 2014) and a senior editor for Harlequin Books since 1997. She lived in Connecticut, Ohio, France, and New Mexico before moving to New York City and the wild world of romance publishing. Patience found her Prince Charming in her forties, which shows that, as in Harlequin's novels, true love can strike at any time.

Everything Is Perfect

Elisabeth Staab

Wedding days are so full of moving parts, so full of things that can go wrong, it's no wonder tensions run high. We all want that big day to be perfect. The best and most important realization I had on my wedding day is that no matter what occurs, everything already *is* perfect. Really.

I like to think of my wedding day as a comedy of errors. Nobody stood up and tried to stop the wedding. No scary secrets popped out of the woodwork at the last second. No explosions. But like a Lifetime romantic comedy, so many "gotchas" popped up that my head started to spin.

I got this insane idea *the night before the wedding* that I needed to a) give my bridesmaids handmade gifts and b) bleach my teeth. God forbid my wedding pictures show a less-than-stellar smile. People, if you can cut it from your to-do list, then cut. But, hey, we all want to be perfect! We want our smiles to sparkle! Yeah, well, if I had it to do over again, I'd get a decent night's sleep and just buy my wedding attendants some nice stationery like a normal person. Your wedding day is l-o-n-g and on a good day two hours of sleep is not enough. Thank God for caffeine.

Then there was that crazy tradition of the bride and groom not seeing each other before the wedding. Looking back, I can't figure out why this tradition meant so much to me. I mean, hey, if it means a lot to you, by all means, rock out with your socks out. My husband and I had already bought a house together. In hindsight, I'm not sure what spending the night before our wedding together would have changed. Besides—I love my mother. I do. I also managed to forget that she likes to sleep with the ambient temperature set to roughly that of the inside of most industrial refrigerators. After my night of eleventh-hour crafting and DIY cosmetic dentistry, I froze in the fetal position for two hours. When one of my bridal attendants showed up a couple of hours later, I threw my arms around her and burst into tears. I wasn't only emotional. I desperately sought body heat!

During coffee, my mother and bridal attendants convinced me I was planning to overtip the caterer. I can't swear to it, but this may have induced what I will forever refer to as "mustard-gate." See below.

Fast-forward to the phone call while we were getting hair and makeup done that my grandfather had been left sitting on my porch unattended with no clue where to go. I'm still not sure how that happened. Making sure you know how everybody is getting *to* the wedding is *key*. Having a person who's willing to run miscellaneous errands, such as picking up your grandparents from your front porch while you're getting your hair shellacked? Priceless.

So is having a fiancé who calls you in the middle of everything to let you know he loves you. Deep breaths. See? Everything is okay.

Then there was the guy who didn't want to give me my dress. *My dress.* I'd bought an off-the-rack sample from one of those ritzy boutiques. A dress that normally sells for thousands I got for a steal, because it had been tried on a bazillion times and the straps were busted. I took it to a restoration place to get it cleaned and repaired, but when the guy realized there were four of us crammed into my tiny car, he didn't want to give up the newly restored gown. "It'll wrinkle," he protested. Luckily, I didn't have to whack him with my new helmet hair, and we all got away without any misdemeanors.

We had a somber and emotional moment when traffic stopped on the way to the venue to allow a motorcade for a fallen police officer to pass. I think this was the moment I realized I really just had to surrender and trust that everything was going to work out. We were already running late. We were getting married on a boat, and it occurred to me then that I'd never explicitly asked whether the boat would leave the dock at the originally scheduled time whether we were ready for it to or not. But a passing funeral, particularly one of a fallen public servant, was more important than me getting into my dress on time. Moreover, it was out of my control. We'd get there as soon as we could, and it would all be okay.

Deeeep breath…

I thought getting married on a boat would be romantic. And it was. What it *also* turned out to be was windy. Even though I tried to warn our florist that the flower arrangements needed to be heavily weighted, they blew over and couldn't be used. I wanted to dress like a princess that day, complete with long, gorgeous, cathedral veil, which almost blew overboard (the veil, not the dress). Those veils catch the wind like nothing you've ever seen, let me tell you. Thank goodness for my maid of honor's fast reflexes. My dress whipped around my feet so much I stepped on the hem and almost tripped and fell over while walking down the aisle.

But, hey, I got there! I was so happy to see the man I loved I almost kissed him too early, and I got totally tripped up on what was supposed to happen when, but whatever. I cried so hard that I dripped snot in front of all our friends and family! It's cool, right? I'm sure nobody noticed. Maybe. Ha.

We did this wine ceremony where we poured two kinds of wine together and drank them to symbolize the mingling of our lives. Since we had the ceremony outside, a fly had the chance to swoop in and *die* in our wine right before we drank. To this day, my husband thinks I'm a big wussy because you can hear me dramatically whisper, "There's a bug in it!" on our wedding video, but damn it, when you encounter a fly legs-up in your wine, it throws you. I still sipped, thank you very much, but I wasn't about to take a big swig and risk swallowing a dead fly. Still, I loved this moment so much that I later wrote it into the mating ceremony of one of my novels. What started as a funny and slightly horrifying moment has stuck with me all these years as a reminder that we could face anything together.

Back to the romance that is getting married on a boat. During our first dance, the boat hit a wave created by a larger boat. Everybody braced for impact, and Tom and I almost fell over. It worked out okay. He grabbed me tight, we found our rhythm again, and his best man made catcalls about how Tom couldn't wait to get me to the hotel room. Everybody laughed, and what could have been embarrassing was funny, and sweet.

Perfect.

Because, so what if a bug died in my wine? So what if I had to clutch my veil for dear life to keep it from blowing overboard? So what if we had to tell people not to bring gifts on board the boat due to Homeland Security? So what if I got yelled at by the ship's captain for trying to head to the top deck before the groomsmen were in position? So what if everyone nearly *fell over* during the first dance? So what if I forgot the moves to "The Time Warp," and my guests were royally confused about the fact that one of my attendants was a) a dude and b) not gay?

Oh. And then there was "mustard-gate." During the reception, my new brother-in-law came over to angrily inform us that the dipping sauce for the chicken nuggets on the kids' meals was not honey mustard but hot mustard. Like the eye-searing stuff you get in Chinese restaurants? So I do feel terrible about all the horrifyingly hot mustard sauce and wonder to this day if it was caterer retaliation for getting a low tip. I'm sorry, kids. Luckily there were few children in attendance, and even fewer who tried the dipping sauce.

At the end of it all, none of it matters except saying "I do" to the person you love. Well…we did have a really nice cake. It said, "Today I marry my friend." And I did.

Honestly, though, I think whether you have a thousand people or none, whether it all goes right or nothing does, if you can just be glad to be together you're golden.

We did choose to have our ceremony outside. I remember being grateful we had sun, because the days leading up had been dreary. Rainy. Cold. I felt like God smiled on us that day, and that was really all we needed. We had the sunshine and each other. What else did we really need?

All the flubs and mishaps got ironed out. I could have really gone insane over them, but saying, "It'll be okay," and focusing on what *was* right worked out pretty well. Because the reality was, it was already perfect.

I got to tell the man who seems to "get" me like nobody else how much I loved him in front of everybody. I got to hear him tell me I was beautiful, and for all my insecurities, *that day* I really believed him. I got to marry my best friend.

Yes, the reception started thirty minutes late, possibly due to the late arrival of the bride and the Dress Nazi. No, the boat didn't leave without us.

Everything was perfect.

Elisabeth Staab still lives with her nose in a book and at least one foot in an imaginary world. She believes that all kinds of safe and sane love should be celebrated, but she adores the fantasy-filled realm of paranormal romance the best. She lives in Northern Virginia with her family and one big scaredy cat where she loves to spend time with good friends, good music, good beverages, and good books (when she isn't making characters fall in love, that is). She digs cats, coffee, sexy stories, and friendly things that go bump in the night.

Visit Elisabeth online at www.elisabethstaab.com.

Holding Out for a Hero

Leslie Carroll

In February 2006, I decided to take control of my romantic destiny. Divorced for a decade, I had spent the preceding few years in a long-distance relationship that, as the months went on, grew more distant in every way. This wasn't how I'd pictured spending the so-called best years of my life. I wanted to wake up next to the man I loved every morning. The only problem was, evidently, I hadn't yet met That Guy. It was time to reclaim my self-esteem.

So I ended the stagnant relationship. Then I did something that one of my heroines might have done, but I'd ordinarily not have had the chutzpah to do myself. In fact, the heroine of my first published novel, *Miss Match,* did do something similar. Kitty Lamb enrolled with a matchmaking service. *I* joined an Internet dating site, under the safety of the pseudonym "romancenovelist."

I've always believed that by expressing your desires aloud, you can make them manifest. So I put words out into the ether.

I enrolled for only one month—not because I expected a Happily Ever After within thirty days, but as an exercise more than anything else. The format for creating my Internet profile allowed me to focus on where I was at that stage in my romantic life, where I'd been, and where it was I truly wanted to be instead. How could I find the right man if I had lost myself? My goal was to become emotionally healthy again after dwelling too long in Doormat Land.

"I give all for love," I wrote in the "About Me" section, adding that I was "seeking a truly chivalrous (though playful) man, honorable and unafraid of commitment. No 'fair weather' romantics, please!" I warned. "I don't want a man who tends to 'fall off the planet' when I need him most—in the moment of jubilation when I want to share my joy and successes with him; and in those moments of disappointment and despair when I need his strength."

In the "I Am Looking For" essay, I said that I sought a man who was "true to his word," having been burned by those who weren't, yearning to meet "a giver, not a taker."

"Can you be as 'real' as you are romantic?" I asked. "Even Lord Byron should not be allergic to cleaning up after himself, have no problem putting the toilet seat back down, and be capable of having a truly honest conversation about anything. Mutually nurturing; we are each other's best friend, each other's rock, each other's greatest fan. We each appreciate the importance of a vital, monogamous sex life to a lasting relationship."

I didn't care if I seemed to be asking for the moon. How could I ever hope to find the right guy if I was dishonest about who I was and what I needed?

My technical skills being fairly limited, the only photo that I managed to upload successfully to my profile was the one my mother had nicknamed "*Vogue* meets *Field & Stream*," taken during my first of perhaps three-ever fly-fishing excursions. There I am in waders, a plaid shirt and fleece jacket, Jackie O sunglasses, and a fur hat, proudly displaying on my line a rainbow trout (which, seconds after this photo op, was safely released).

I worried about that picture. Guys who expected to meet a real outdoorswoman might be dismayed to discover that I consider "roughing it" the furthest room from the pool, that I view nature as a spectator sport and will run only for a crosstown bus. But it was the only recent photo that flattered me, and it wasn't a total misrepresentation. It showed that I was willing to try new things, wade out of my comfort zone—while retaining my own identity, at least from the neck up!

Five days after I joined the Internet dating site, on February 17, 2006, I received a lengthy e-mail from "sunshine42day."

> DEAR RN(A MEDIC FOR THE HEART?)
>
> [AND I THINK: *This is promising; he has a sense of humor.*]
>
> I TAKE INTEGRITY OVER ALLEGIANCE, PASSION OVER THE PRIDE IN THE EFFORT OVER EXPEDIENT SLOPPINESS. I MEASURE MYSELF NOT BY THE EYES OF OTHERS, BUT BY THE FACE I SEE DAILY IN THE MIRROR. I AM KIND, GENTLE, AND LOVING BUT NOT WEAK. I AM PREPARED TO LEAD BUT EQUALLY READY TO FOLLOW, A TENDER HEART AND A TRUSTING SOUL. I GREATLY EXCEED THE THRESHOLD FOR LEAVING THE TOILET SEAT DOWN. FOR YOU: DOES YOUR WARDROBE INCLUDE BLACK DRESS TO HIKING BOOTS, DO YOU AGREE THERE CANNOT BE TOO MANY HUGS SHARED BETWEEN LOVED ONES, AND THAT ANYTHING CAN BE DISCUSSED BECAUSE THE DESIRE FOR A RELATIONSHIP CAN TRUMP WHATEVER CHALLENGE—WHEN THERE IS COMPLETE COMMUNICATION? PLEASE LET ME KNOW IF YOU'D WELCOME ANOTHER NOTE.

He signed it from a location that I knew to be a major war zone—a hotbed, in fact—then added, "(BTW: I had to write this note four times to have it sent—a poor satellite signal.)"

Well! Someone who wanted to meet me so much that he retyped his letter of introduction four times merited a reply. Not only that, there was not one typo, not a single misspelling, and it was grammatically perfect. You laugh. But with an online name like "romancenovelist," it was shocking how many men addressed a woman who clearly valued the written word with "Yo!" or "Hey!" followed by a string of incoherent, rambling, badly spelled sentences.

Not so, sunshine42day, aka Scott. According to his profile, his ideal relationship was a "commitment to communicate, honesty, respect, loyalty, affection, and shared values." So far he was batting a thousand with me. "I am not perfect, but I try, and I seek a woman with flaws that can mesh with mine. If you want to know more, you'll have to write."

Write I did. Marveling at how he had somehow found me from a remote base on the front lines where he was the chief, in charge of hundreds of men of more than one nationality. Especially when I had stated that, after an unsuccessful long-distance relationship, I was looking to meet a guy who lived within five miles of the Upper West Side of Manhattan!

Scott was divorced, with a teenage son who lived with his mother. A nonsmoking native Californian, he described himself as "athletic," and we shared the same tastes in music and old movie classics. Our religious backgrounds were similar. He had checked off the same cultural "likes" I had, although he was a *lot* more outdoorsy. Little black dress to hiking boots? (I *did* own a pair from those few fly-fishing excursions.) Yes, but not worn at the same time, I told him, or I would look like a Fashion Week victim.

Within twenty-four hours we had exchanged private e-mail addresses. A few days later, we closed our memberships with the online dating site to pursue a correspondence on our own. We had already lived and loved enough to be able to learn from our failures, to admit the mistakes of our pasts so that this time we would not repeat them with each other.

Like the heroines and heroes of the epistolary romances of the eighteenth and nineteenth centuries, and so many of their real-life counterparts whose courtships were restricted to correspondence, our letters chronicled our love story as it unfolded. Because half a world separated us with no hope of meeting in person until he received leave to return to the States for a few days the following month, our exchanges were limited to words and a few photographs.

We told each other everything, writing several times a day in long, single-spaced e-mails. The day after his introductory note, Scott impressed me with his literary knowledge, making a reference to Nathaniel Hawthorne's poignantly ironic short story "The Great Stone Face." His e-mail ended with the words:

Kind words supported by deeds,
should be no surprise,
and accepted with grace
for two who love one another.

Under the poem he added, ("just something that popped up as a thought—thought I'd share it.")

Love? Had I met my match already? It was too soon. Things were happening so fast. *Be careful what you wish for*, said the angel on my shoulder. Or was it a little imp?

So I wanted to make sure Scott saw my "flaws," too. I told him how busy I was, how many hours I spent at the computer researching and writing. Maybe I was pushing him away because I was frightened. "And, oh, I still sleep with the toy stuffed bunny I've had since I was three months old," I added, "and my twenty-year-old teddy bear." Making sure he understood, and was prepared to accept my whimsy. "Love me, love my bunny (and my bear)," I cautioned.

That's okay, he replied. "To act like responsible adults, and feel the exuberance of childhood, that should stay with us."

After a week of copious correspondence, *I had to hear his voice*. I still had no idea how he sounded. Tenor or baritone? Did he lisp? Because all the guys on the base shared only two phones, Scott had to reserve it. On the appointed evening, nearly two weeks after our first e-mail, I answered the phone on the first ring. The delay of a few seconds while the connection kicked in seemed like an eternity. Scott sounded gentle and kind. His voice was soft. I wondered what side of him his buddies and subordinates saw. At one point, we both began crying from the sheer joy of being able to have a conversation. We take so much for granted every day that you fail to realize what a treat a simple phone call can be to someone posted to a remote part of the world, with little time or opportunity to connect with his loved ones.

We made plans to meet in New York City during his leave. Meanwhile, we would maintain our daily correspondence and speak over the phone as often as he could call.

Only six days into our epistolary romance, Scott had begun dropping innuendos into his letters. Three weeks after we exchanged our first online greeting, he was certain he wanted to marry me. On March 2, he wrote: "We are soul mates."

This rapidity of affection happens to characters in romance novels and, in a famous observation of Mr. Darcy's, not to real people. It was hard for me to conceive that my life was quickly emulating an implausible plotline. I was on the verge of obtaining my heart's desire—yet at the same time, was terrified of the prospect.

I admitted that I had emerged battle-scarred from the minefields of romance. Scott's exuberance scared me. As easy as it would have been for me to begin redecorating castles in the air, now I was slowing down through all the yellow lights. Perhaps he didn't deserve such prudence. But how could I be certain I wasn't rushing into anything I would later regret?

He had been planning to transfer to New York City after this overseas tour. Our next step was to get engaged. But you've never *met* each other, our friends and relatives insisted. My literary agent and my best friends warned that he could be an ax murderer for all I knew. Convinced that I must be a gold digger, Scott's sisters scolded him for having a too trusting heart.

Was this really my life? Signing on to The Knot Web site to scope out wedding-dress silhouettes less than a month after posting my dating profile online?

I sent him care packages through a U.S. Army address. I was surprised with gifts of impossibly gorgeous arrangements from Belle Fleur in Chelsea. Several continents away, Scott had researched the most romantic florist in New York City. When I told him about my visit to The Jewish Museum to see a Sarah Bernhardt exhibit, he began to call me his "faraway princess," a reference to Bernhardt's eponymous role in Edmond Rostand's 1895 romance *La Princesse Lointaine*.

During enemy shelling, while the men were hunkered inside a bunker, as mortars rained down about them, he took my photo, lovingly protected by a plastic sleeve, from his pocket and showed it to a colleague, in rapture about the woman he had decided to marry.

On March 14, I received the following e-mail:

> I mentioned in my last that I was just about to head off to a meeting with my teammates, and that I still had a few tears in my eyes. I managed to clear away the tears, at least so they were not so visible (and I was aided by the dark bunker we meet in), and towards the end of the meeting, I made an announcement. After I finished the morning briefing/plans portion, and others provided their contributions, I asked for alibis (this is the time for others to bring up related but not critical mission essential issues), and after that was done, it was my turn. I told them I found my soul mate, was in love, wanted to marry this woman, and by the way, she had a write-up in the "Daily Variety" about her book, Play Dates, being picked up by an entertainment production company. There was silence, and I adjourned the meeting. Afterwards, four of the fellows came up to me and noted that the Global War on Terror (GWOT) stopped for a romantic moment, maybe for the first time, at least they had observed, in their service abroad since late 2001. They were serious, and what was important, they appreciated that it was OK to show a vulnerable side, and although not stated, it was acknowledged that it was a beautiful thing to see romance, thoughtfulness and hope, in a rough and tumble environment. It was heartening because they must have had their own similar thoughts of love back home or hopefulness for

those who would like something more than the satisfaction they get in places like this. Like a lot of things, it is good to get some things out in the open, and I did, and maybe just for a moment, at least in the minds of my men, they had a reminder that beyond this war and Spartan life we lead here, the beauty of romance and love is cradled within, and protected by the brutalities of war. A little moment, in a faraway place, you were a part of it, you make this possible, and all this happened probably while you slept. You see, the magical effect you have on me, us and maybe even for others too. We'll continue to lead by example, and do so together. I love you.

Later that month, I received a phone call from the office of The Players, the social club on Gramercy Park founded in 1888 by actor Edwin Booth. Although I was the first woman to become a third-generation member, financial constraints had compelled me to take a leave of absence. "Your dues have been paid through the end of the year," I was informed. My benefactor wished to remain anonymous. I felt like Pip in *Great Expectations*. But, seriously, there was more than one person who could have stepped into the breach. It might have been my mentor. "I don't want to thank the wrong person," I told the club. "It would be mortifying. Just tell me the location from which the call was placed."

Scott.

And finally—at the end of March, we met in person! He got off the elevator in my apartment building, dragging his enormous black "pelican" suitcase. I stood in the open doorway, not wanting to wait a moment longer to see his face, to finally hold him in my arms. Our first kiss lasted forty-five minutes. The nickel tour of my apartment began in the bedroom.

And he was just as handsome and winning and kind in the flesh.

But then came a bombshell I had never anticipated.

Scott's teenage son also had to meet me. His son had not gotten along with his ex-stepmother. Much as he loved me and wanted to marry me, Scott didn't want his kid to endure another uncomfortable domestic situation.

I felt as though I had been sucker punched. Blindsided. I couldn't imagine our future being in the hands of a third party who was not going to live under our roof anyway. *Of course* I wanted a positive and healthy relationship with his son. But I didn't want to be judged.

Happily, for all of us, Scott's son and I got along terrifically. A few days later, Scott's overseas deployment resumed. Every time he had to leave the base, my heart was in my mouth. Now, my future husband was out there putting his life on the line for our country, braving enemy fire.

On the evening of June 7, less than four months from our first online exchange, Scott returned to the States. The following day he got on bended knees, both of them, at The Players club and proposed to me. The engagement ring was no surprise. At his behest, I had chosen it myself from a SoHo jeweler while he was still overseas. It took all of nine seconds to select my wedding gown at Macy's, having already decided on the style from all those visits to The Knot.

We were married at The Players on May 19, 2007. The image on our homemade wedding invitations was Sarah Bernhardt as *La Princesse Lointaine*. One of the original posters from her production hangs on our wall. It was a foregone conclusion that our wedding recessional would be the traditional march from Mendelssohn's *A Midsummer Night's Dream,* not only because it's gorgeous and uplifting, but also because I am a descendant of the composer. And, with a grin on my face, I had walked—no, nearly danced—down the aisle toward my groom, to the accompaniment of a rather *un*traditional selection: Bonnie Tyler belting out Jim Steinman and Dean Pitchford's kick-ass anthem from the 1980s, "Holding Out for a Hero."

Leslie Carroll is the author of several works of historical nonfiction and women's fiction, and, under the pen names Juliet Grey and Amanda Elyot, is a multipublished author of historical fiction.  She is also a classically trained professional actress and an award-winning audio book narrator. A frequent commentator on royal romances and relationships, Leslie has been interviewed by numerous broadcast, online, and print media, and appears on the Canadian History Channel series "The Secret Life Of ..." Leslie and her husband, Scott, divide their time between New York City and Washington, DC.

Visit Leslie online at www.lesliecarroll.com.

Part III

How We Love

Pasta for Dinner

Suzan Colón

"*I*'m thinking of writing a book."

In order to tell the story of my own romance, I have to tell the story of how I became a romance writer, and for that I need to point out when I said this to my husband. Fall 2008. Venerable financial institutions were collapsing. Banks were cutting off credit; people were rushing to withdraw money and hide it under their mattresses. Publishing houses were freezing book submissions because they couldn't pay advances.

Perhaps not the best time for me, a recently laid-off magazine writer, to announce that my backup plan in this economic maelstrom was to become an author.

I braced myself for Nathan's reaction and mentally called up my bullet-pointed list of reasons that now was the time for me to write a book at long last. I had trouble getting past the first and only point: There were no job or freelance prospects. There was nothing to do but try the riskiest proposition of all.

I didn't have to worry about the points and their high-feebleness factor. Nathan, being the logical person who I sometimes lovingly call Spock, asked me what kind of book. A memoir, I said, sounding crazy even to myself. A book about finding my grandmother's recipes and making them with my mother as she told me the stories of how our family got through hard times. As hard as this recession and worse.

And in this time of dramatic and drastic uncertainty, when we, too, had taken money out of the bank to hide it in case of further economic collapse, at a time when our income had been slashed in half with the loss of my job, Nathan said something that carried me that day and since. It's a sentence that has come to rival *I love you* and *Will you marry me?* in spoken proof of love. He said, "Go for it. I know you can do this."

Most people think the challenge in writing a book is actually sitting down and writing it. That's never been my case. I've been in love with writing since the day I stayed home from Miss Maggenheim's fourth-grade class with a cold and tried to write a short story about a goldfish and a teddy bear trading places. I never got to the predictable moral of this little fable because I was thwarted by the mechanics of Mom's typewriter (in that sense, the hardest part was actually sitting down and writing the story). But writing would be my first exposure to passion, and eventually heartbreak, but always love.

I didn't realize what a natural outgrowth writing was from my voracious reading habit. Childhood tales of teddy bears grew into teenage curiosity about love, and I discovered romance novels. *Ooooh.* They had the slightly forbidden sheen of adult reading due to the sexy parts, but they promised and delivered princes falling in love with flawed girls who then became princesses. (Being a tall, bucktoothed, Coke-bottle-glasses-wearing teenager, the draw was obvious.)

Seeing how much I liked these novels and hoping I might one day gravitate toward some sort of career choice, my mother bought me a book about how to write romances. "You could do this," she said. My small world, which consisted of reading love stories and mooning over Scottish pop stars The Bay City Rollers, burst open. I could write about love? I could write, period? At the time I didn't even know writing was an actual vocation. I don't know what I thought, but my mother had possibilities dancing in her eyes.

I did become a writer, though I took a path that requires less faith and more fortitude, and occasionally more wine. I became a rock journalist.

Again, I didn't know this was an actual vocation. At the time I was a naïve young woman who'd been enrolled in business school by an exasperated mother whose kid just wouldn't latch on to anything other than reading music magazines.

I resented the hell out of business school and its dress code of skirts Monday to Thursday and, oh joy, dress slacks on Friday. TGIPF, Thank God It's Pants Friday. But I learned how to type eighty-five words a minute, which got my foot and fast hands in the door of a music magazine that needed an intern. Two months later, I was hired as an assistant editor, for an annual salary of fifteen thousand dollars. My job was to interview rock stars for a living and write about it. That I would be paid on top of that? I thought the world had gone mad in my favor. I was rich.

If this were a movie instead of an essay, cue the whirlwind montage: our heroine interviewing rock stars backstage and on the tour bus. Janet Jackson, Aerosmith, Duran Duran. Then she's laid off and migrates to a teen magazine. Christian Slater and…well, stars whose names I can't even remember now because they've been crowded out by the names of my fictional romance heroes. But I'm getting ahead of myself. The montage continues with two common themes: writing for magazines and getting laid off in recessions.

It's an equation well known to anyone who works in this area of the publishing business. In times of economic trouble, people cut back, and small luxuries are the first to go. Manipedis, pricey coffees and magazines. Sales go down and so does the head count. Over my twenty-four-year career in magazines, I went through three recessions and was laid off, along with many others, each time.

Something in me had gotten brittle, so when bent just a tad too far, there was a small splintering noise audible only to me. I refused to be laid off again. I was now in business for myself.

This decision might not have had the ring of a declaration if I hadn't been married at the time.

I say that not from the more financially secure position of having a second income in the house. By the time I'd met Nathan at a yoga retreat in Costa Rica, I'd gone rogue many times and always managed to make ends meet. In the career stability sense, he and I were opposites. He'd been a mechanical contractor for the same company for over twenty years. I was on a cycle of working at a magazine for a few years and going freelance for a few years, usually after I was laid off. Like now.

The last time I lost my job we had pasta for dinner. It's one of those details you latch on to in order to keep your hands from shaking. The recession, the loss of my job, the bleakness of the future, all of it was making me sip the air like a drowning woman. *Ravioli*, I thought. *We're having cheese ravioli, I'm forty-five years old and magazines are going to hell in a handbasket and I'm never going to get hired again and I can't do this anymore and what will Nathan say and I think I'll just heat up the sauce now.*

Over this dinner, I told Nathan I'd been laid off. I also told him I was going into business for myself, freelancing where and when I could. And he said, "That's probably a good idea, with jobs being so scarce. You'll find work." Never have I sighed so gratefully. Never has overcooked pasta seemed such a banquet.

Months later, when that work hadn't materialized, I went to the edge of the diving board again and put forth my plan to write a book. At the time it was a bit like saying I was going to jump off that diving board and hope there was water, or anything, waiting for me below.

My husband asked me the questions that showed he was listening, and that he cared, and that demonstrated the truth of the idea that couples are made of puzzle pieces that fit together. He's practical, and I leap off diving boards.

An integral part of any leap is faith. On that night, as he has on a few nights since, Nathan looked at me and said, "I know you can do this."

There's an old philosophical question: If a tree falls in the forest and no one is there to hear it, does it make a sound? Authors ask themselves a variation on that theme. What if I write a book and no one reads it?

Absent a legion of devoted fans and a publisher enthusiastically asking about the next book, a writer lives on faith. This can be a thin meal. I work alone, as most writers do. Now that I write romantic fiction, I spend large amounts of time in a world inside my head. After a while, the weeds of doubt spring up in the garden. *Can I do this? Will it be successful?* The struggles of romance heroines often bring tears to a reader's eyes because they're so true to life. My guess is that authors weave their own feelings, including fears, into material that becomes the flesh of their characters.

My own faith gets words onto a page. Before a single word is written, though, sometimes I look down from my diving board. My aspirations may be so high I get dizzy.

But if I look carefully, I'll see a handsome man with black hair and cool eyeglasses. Knowing him, he's got a tape measure and something to gauge wind velocity and the depth of the water I'm about to dive into.

Then he looks up at me. And he smiles.

Suzan Colón is the author of the novel *Beach Glass* and the memoir *Cherries in Winter: My Family's Recipe for Hope in Hard Times*. She has also written three young adult novels. Suzan lives with her husband, Nathan, and two demanding cats in New Jersey.

Visit her at www.suzancolon.net.

Catch Me When I Fall

Sara Jane Stone

The first time, I was getting off the subway in Midtown Manhattan. I remember the exhaustion. I was so tired. But I only had to climb one set of stairs to reach the busy city street. I made it to the top, and my water broke.

Fear pushed me into denial. This wasn't happening. Not yet. My due date was a month away. I went to the nearest Starbucks, locked myself in the bathroom and called my husband.

White knights come in many guises. Mine arrived in a yellow cab and delivered me safely to the hospital. He stayed with me through the first night, easing my fears. After a week on hospital bed rest, I went into active labor, and my son arrived. Five pounds, twelve ounces, he was perfect for a few blissful moments. And then he couldn't breathe.

The doctors rushed my newborn into surgery, repairing his collapsed lung. The next time I saw him, a machine was helping him breathe. Still dizzy from giving birth, I sat by his incubator and wept. My husband was at my side. He'd been there the entire time, only leaving to check with doctors and secure a room for me.

"Sing to him," he said. "He'll recognize your voice."

I opened the door to the incubator and sang "You Are My Sunshine." My husband held my hand. Knowing I was terrified, he helped me find my way through my fear. He must have been scared, too, but he stayed strong, so amazingly strong in a way that had nothing to do with muscles. In that sad, scary moment, singing to my baby who couldn't breathe, I knew I was loved.

Five days later, I turned thirty and brought my son home from the hospital. Weeks turned into months, and my son grew, healthy and strong. I adjusted to life as a stay-at-home mom. My husband, my white knight in a yellow cab, was by my side where he has been for the last eleven years. I called him when I needed help or had a bad day. Just as I had in the days before and after our son's birth, I gave him all of my emotions—the pain, the frustration, the fear—and he handed me back love, every day without fail.

The second time, nineteen months after my son arrived, I was sitting on the couch watching television with my husband. I was seven months pregnant. And my water broke.

This time I did not have to call. He was right there. But the fear—it was so much greater. I wept. I told him over and over, "I don't want to lose this baby."

At the same time, I didn't want to leave my son. He was still a baby in so many ways. And I wasn't ready to leave for the hospital. Not yet. The holidays were approaching. We didn't have our tree yet. Decorating it as a family—that was important to me. Seeing my son's face on Christmas morning, I didn't want to miss that lying in a hospital bed. As my fear rose, all of these seemingly trivial details grew until they left me paralyzed.

My husband took charge, calling my midwife and our neighbor to come watch my son. He drove me from our home in Brooklyn to the hospital in Manhattan. He took care of me. He pushed me past the fear.

Days later, while I was lying in my hospital bed on the high-risk maternity ward, my husband went out and bought the most beautiful tree I'd ever seen. When my nineteen-month-old son woke up the following morning, he shouted with joy, "Tree! Tree!" My husband recorded the moment and sent me the video. The tree stood in our apartment, undecorated, a visible sign that our holiday plans had taken a detour but were not forgotten.

I used my time in the hospital to finish the manuscript that would eventually, after many rounds of revisions, become my first published book, *Command Performance*. I sent it off to my agent on December 12, in the afternoon. Hours later, I gave birth to my baby girl. She was tiny, only three pounds, thirteen ounces. But she could breathe. She was healthy and beautiful.

I was discharged the next day, returning home to my son, my husband, and our bare tree. Over the next few weeks, we juggled trips to the NICU to visit our daughter, still too small to come home; holiday plans; and our son, whose world had changed overnight. We decorated the tree. Together.

We took shifts at the hospital. I would leave in the morning to hold and nurse our little girl, while my husband stayed home. The subway ride was a nightmare. I was in limbo between the child I felt needed me at home and the one waiting for me in the incubator. I cried from the minute I stepped onto the train until I walked through the doors to the hospital. My hormones, still in turmoil from the birth, did not help. I probably looked like a crazy person, with the hospital bands still on my arms, wearing my maternity clothes even though I'd had the baby (nothing else fit, so I had no choice) and my face streaming with tears.

After a week, I couldn't bear it anymore. I picked up a romance novel and, for the forty-five-minute ride between my two children, I lost myself in the story. The characters in the books loved deeply and openly, their emotions often running the gamut from head-over-heels to heartbreak at that black moment when they thought all was lost. Long after we brought my daughter home, I continued to read. I carried my e-reader while I walked in circles around my bedroom for hours each night, hoping my little girl would finally stop crying and fall asleep, losing myself in the magic of first love.

There is something enchanting about falling in love. Everything is fresh and new. It's this magic that draws readers to romance novels—that, and the fact that the sex is amazing, if not the first time, then by the end of the book. The heroes, nine times out of ten—at least in most of the stories I read and write—have jaw-dropping muscles. There are obstacles, sure. Some seem insurmountable. But in the end, love triumphs. Always.

But in real life, the happy ending does not stop there. The obstacles continue, changing over time, even when the muscles fade. But I've found that love grows. And it changes. No longer new and shiny, it becomes dependable.

That is not a sexy word. But after eleven years together and two beautiful children (who try my patience daily), dependable is everything. It is the person you call when you are so afraid you don't know your next step. Dependable is the person who will catch you when you fall, always and forever, when you need saving the most.

My white knight still brings me flowers for no reason. He whisks me away for surprise nights away from the kids. The romance is present in our lives. And I'm grateful for that. I cherish his efforts to make me feel special and hope I'm able to do the same for him.

But when asked how we love, I do not think about the flowers and nights spent alone in a hotel. I think about how my husband was there for me when I needed him most. When I was scared. When I was falling.

When I think about how we love, I think about the Christmas tree waiting, undecorated, because he knew that spending the time to hang the ornaments together meant something to me. I think about the man who told me to sing to my newborn, knowing that it would help us both.

How do we love now? As a family. One I can depend on always and forever.

Sara Jane Stone currently resides in Brooklyn, New York, with her very supportive real-life hero, two lively young children, and a lazy Burmese cat. Her first book, *Command Performance*, released in 2013. In summer 2014, she will release *Command Control* (published by Harlequin Blaze) and *Full Exposure* (published by Avon Impulse).

Visit Sara Jane online at www.sarajanestone.com.

Real Life & Real Love

Katharine Ashe

He was tall, dark and handsome, and everybody said so. Women would stop me on the street, lean into my shoulder and whisper to me how gorgeous he was. Men did it, too, but they didn't whisper. They looked slightly askance, as if they couldn't quite handle it, squared their shoulders defensively and said things like, "That's a really good-looking guy."

Admittedly, I was proud. I liked this adulation-by-association. As a bedraggled graduate student with too many bills to pay, too much work to do, never enough sleep, and bags perpetually beneath my eyes, I enjoyed being partnered with a specimen of perfect masculine beauty.

The only one who wasn't impressed was my husband. For my Tall Dark and Handsome was not, after all, him.

My husband—who was in fact tall, dark and very good-looking, to the extent that on our second date I dubbed him "Dreamboat"—never wanted a dog. But I did. I'd been longing for a dog pretty much since I'd been alive. Now, for the first time in my nomadic life, I anticipated several unbroken years of residence in the US, and I knew this was the moment to go for it. When one night out by a lake in Michigan in a house overrun by puppies we met the beautiful creature that I later named Atlas, my husband would not, however, commit. Faced with this intransigence, I picked up that ebony satin pup with floppy ears and long legs, put him in the car and said, "We're keeping him."

Atlas grew up to be a stunner: ninety-five pounds, a cross between a Lab and Dane, all legs and deep chest and noble face and expressive golden eyes. Since everybody in our posh neighborhood (in which we lived in a tiny attic apartment) had purebred dogs and always asked us about his breed, we invented one just for the silliness of it. He was a Danish Short-Haired Viborg Hound, we would say, impossible to get unless you had a personal connection with the breeder in Europe. Then we would giggle as we told the truth: that Atlas was actually a true American, i.e. a mutt.

Tall Dark and Handsome was a handful. Much more than a handful, in fact. He was excessively energetic, rambunctious, ferociously loving, devoted, squirrel-crazy, constantly hungry, exhaustingly emotionally needy, and smart enough to want to explore the world but apparently not smart enough not to try to jump out a third-story window.

It was Atlas's high-maintenance character and my tendency to indulge it that my husband found a tad difficult to bear. We had been together for seven years, and some of those years we'd spent across oceans from each other. Now we were finally living together in the same place and commuting seventy miles to teach at a university where my husband had been offered a full-time job while I finished up my degree. He didn't want to have to worry about a troublesome puppy. He didn't want to hear from our landlord about how Atlas barked for an hour after we drove away in the morning. He didn't want to *not* go on a whim to the beach for a weekend or fly to Europe for a few weeks, because Atlas—with his nervous disposition—would inevitably lose five pounds for every day spent in a kennel. My husband didn't want to have to walk the dog in the freezing rain when I couldn't be home in the evening. And, on our junior professor salaries, he wasn't fond of the vet bills either.

A superlatively responsible man in many ways, my husband just didn't want the particular responsibility of a dog.

But I did. Atlas loved me. Completely. All I did was feed and walk and play with him, and in return he gave me unconditional love at any time I needed it and even when I didn't think I needed it but actually did. This, my friends, is a very good arrangement.

So I did my best to take care of my big beautiful pup on my own. I tried not to depend on my husband for Atlas's care, and I worked hard to find suitable arrangements for him when we wanted to travel. I did a pretty good job of it. I loved both of my boys, and I didn't want to give up either.

Wait, you say, *isn't this a book about real-life heroes? Shouldn't you be writing about your husband instead of your devotion to your dog?*

Oh, but I am. Because, you see, though my husband didn't want a dog, he nevertheless loved it simply because I did.

When Atlas was three, my husband told me he was ready to have a baby. I wasn't. At least not entirely. I definitely *wanted* a baby, and I had prayed long and sincerely about it. But contemplating the moment when I would actually make this giant life leap was another thing altogether.

Because I loved my husband and because I wasn't getting any younger, we had a baby.

Miracle. Gift. Blessing. Another perfect male creature to lose my heart to completely, irrevocably, forever and ever. I thanked heaven and my husband and the whole world for this precious person who now graced our lives.

Embarking upon this new and thrilling adventure, I swiftly realized that I had learned a lot about raising a child from raising a high-maintenance dog. I had learned how to put aside my needs and devote myself to another being entirely. I had learned that life is messy and little critters are even messier. I had learned that the ideals in advice books are rarely achieved in reality, but that it didn't matter, because where there was love there was joy.

I also learned that, whereas you cannot easily take a ninety-five-pound dog on a transatlantic flight, you can take a small child on that flight, which made the man in my life very happy. I learned that, while an indifferent dog person, that man was a wonderful father. And I learned that negotiating a trio of males who rarely shared the same needs took patience, care and hard work.

One of my responses to this challenge was to look for a companion for Atlas. I found Idaho on a farm: a tiny ball of brown fur with a tail like a rat, who waddled around like a piglet. We fell in love instantly.

Unsurprisingly, my husband said, "Are you insane? We have a baby, two jobs and the highest-maintenance dog in America, and you want *another dog*?"

I said, "Yes. We need her."

He said, "No. We don't."

So I brought her home. She fell in love with my boys, and now we were five.

Fast-forward, if you will, through a decade during which my husband thrived at work, my publishing career took off, and our son grew from a miracle into an even bigger miracle.

Then one deceptively bright day beneath a brilliant blue sky—one horrible day—I held Atlas in my arms as his noble soul traveled on to another place. Shortly after that, both my husband and I experienced health problems. Two months later, my father-in-law passed away. Three months later, my mother got sick.

It was a dark year, the worst time of my adult life.

Then, just as my husband and I were crawling out of the devastation of that year and beginning to see the sun again, something else happened in our family. Something worse. And this time it affected our son, too.

I cannot specify the details of it here, but at that time I saw that nothing had prepared me—or us—for this. None of the parenting we had practiced, none of the lessons we had learned, none of the challenges we had faced could help us weather this new storm. It was a new, cruel kind of time for us, not a time of quiet grief and coping, but a time of tearing apart, of pain and confusion and even fear. It was a time in which we were tested beyond anything we had known before or imagined, a time in which on the outside we held it together, because that's what you do when you have jobs and responsibilities and people who depend on you, while on the inside we crumbled.

Not very long ago—so recently in fact that I can still sense the edge of shadows as I write this now—our situation altered significantly for the better, and the sun finally peeked out from behind the clouds. We could see the light again. We could feel it on our hesitantly upturned faces. I began to suspect that we might, in fact, weather this storm. That perhaps, in fact, we already had. For it seemed that while my husband and I hadn't been paying close attention to our relationship, love had enabled us to endure, indeed to triumph.

When I say that love enabled us to triumph, I don't refer to the heady love that once inspired the nickname "Dreamboat." Nor do I mean the true love that had led to the birth of our precious child. Nor was it the generous love that had expanded our family to include four-footed friends. This love was different, I realized. This love was deep, rooted in years, in friendship, in shared suffering, and in hope.

The other day I mentioned to my two boys that, for the first time since Atlas's death, I was considering getting a puppy for me and Idaho. My husband turned to me with a gentle, kind smile and said, "That sounds like a really great idea."

Katharine Ashe is the award-winning author of twelve lush, sweeping historical romances set in the British Empire, including *How to Be a Proper Lady*, an Amazon.com Editors' Choice for the Ten Best Books of 2012. A professor of European history, she lives in the wonderfully warm southeast with her husband, son, dog and a garden she likes to call romantic rather than unkempt.

Please visit her at
www.katharineashe.com.

When You Come Home

CARLENE LOVE FLORES

When I was a little girl, Grandma and I would sit at her living room window, waiting and watching. She'd sing me the old folk song "She'll Be Coming 'Round the Mountain" over and over until I'd see them—Mom's headlights pulling into the court late at night after making her way back to me from Vegas. They were always the first things I'd recognize. My parents were divorced, and monthly visits to my dad in San Diego were part of their arrangement. I guess you could say my whole life I've been waiting for someone to come home.

The beauty of being a child was that life to me was a great adventure. The beauty of being an adult is that I now am also grateful, because those back-and-forth trips between Mom and Dad taught me the importance of loving from afar and sharing.

Little did I know how valuable growing up in that way would be.

The day I met my husband, we were outside practicing for an earthquake drill, as is normal in Southern California. I was a freshman, and he was a junior, although we are only one year apart in age. The day of that drill, I knew of Adrian Flores, but that was about it. As I stood on the field, waiting for the okay to go back to class, someone tapped me on the shoulder. When

I turned, Adrian waved, smiled and then walked away. It was my first close-up glimpse of the black-haired, green-eyed young man who would soon become my hero.

There was no way either of us at the tender ages of fifteen and sixteen could have known this manner of our first meeting would be the hallmark of the way we loved for the next twenty-three years.

When Adrian left for the Army on the heels of graduating high school, I was sad but not devastated. After all, I had junior year to think about, and it was kind of cool having a boyfriend in the military. That was the gift I'd been given of youth: the inability to see the big picture. It didn't dawn on me at the time just how much my sweetheart would be missed in the year to come.

Senior year made its debut, and that was when I truly felt like Cinderella without her prince. Another life lesson I learned that year: When you're loving from afar, learn to accept the kindness of those around you even if you're a natural-born hermit like me. I'll always look back at prom and cherish my stand-in date, Jessica.

Separations are tough, but homecomings are the chocolate and chicken soup our hearts and souls need. What a goofy grin a girl will get when she sees her one and only coming through the airport arrival gate. Mine were always pretty darn goofy.

That first year Adrian was gone, I shared him with Oklahoma, Texas and Turkey. No wonder he slept straight through the part of the flight home where he was supposed to de-board in San Diego and run into my arms. Back then, security was more relaxed, and Adrian ended up continuing a little too far north. He tells me his brief stint in San Francisco, where he passed his time at the USO, was memorable for a young soldier. He still remembers the Persian Gulf, Vietnam and World War II vets killing time before their flights alongside him. I don't remember being a very happy nineteen-year-old young woman that night, but now all I can do is smile. Now I've lived enough to know the difference between disappointment and true heartache.

As I learned and experienced and, therefore, became a less-selfish person, always playing catch-up to my husband in that department, it seems sometimes we were tested more because we could handle more.

This time it was me saying goodbye to Mom as I prepared to leave the country. At twenty, landing at Germany's Frankfurt airport was scary. I'd always been good with languages, but my Spanish may well have been Greek as sign after incomprehensible sign made me want to cry. The worst was knowing that Adrian was somewhere in that airport waiting for me—if I could only find the right set of doors to pass through. Desperate, I finally decided to tag along behind a random family who looked like they were as eager as I was to leave the airport. Thankfully, they led me in the right direction.

He was there. So handsome. My husband of four months. God, we were just babies.

And although we'd run off to Vegas four months earlier, our married life started that day. For better or worse, it was him and me, on our own in a foreign country.

Life was like a honeymoon.

When we weren't working and studying, we saw castles and ruins, churches and rivers. We learned what really old was, comparing the thousands of years of European history to the hundreds of years of U.S. history. We drove ridiculously fast on the autobahn in a gold Opel Ascona we'd bought off a man named Ty, who I'm sure sold hoopties to many a newbie couple. We parked our car like the locals did—two wheels on the sidewalk and two on the narrow street, except for the first time I attempted to do it and landed the entire car on the sidewalk. It was one of the first times I'd truly heard Adrian crack up laughing. The embarrassment was worth it. My turn to snicker came the first time we ordered from a German restaurant counter, and Adrian came away with a plate full of potatoes, potatoes and potatoes. That's what he got for ordering by picture. Of course, he had to play it off like that was the best darn meal of his life.

Life was fun. We saw our first snowfall together.

We learned that we were going to have a baby.

Months passed, and one night while we were home watching *90210* reruns on AFN, I knew something was very wrong. In the second trimester, my water shouldn't be breaking, but that's exactly what it felt like. Bewildered, Adrian drove me—five months pregnant—to the military hospital in Landstuhl. I was surprised to learn later that it was only twenty miles away. As you can imagine, it felt much farther from our rural Army post. That night I delivered a tiny, sweet baby boy who had unfortunately already passed on.

This was one of those times I thanked God Adrian was home, because it wasn't always that way when he was a young field artillery soldier. They trained relentlessly as the horrible conflict in Bosnia raged on.

We healed. We tried to move on and believe it was just a fluke thing that had happened.

Pregnant with our second child, while Adrian was away this time on a training mission, I knew something again was not right. I called his unit, but he was unable to make it back. Preferring to wish this all away, I at least had the sense to begrudgingly knock on the door of the woman who lived across the hall and ask for help.

Sandy, a wonderful and kind neighbor I barely knew, drove me to the hospital—six months pregnant. By a miracle, Adrian somehow made it back from the field and to my side just before I gave birth to our second baby boy. The little one weighed nearly two pounds and fit in the palms of our hands. For twelve hours, he fought the bravest of fights, but in the end was just too tiny and passed on.

Sometimes I wonder how long it took Adrian not to fear coming home. Depending on the day, I was either holding it all in or begging to leave the country. I think he wondered on a daily basis when I might lose it. But he kept coming home, being the strong one, and we got through those last two months overseas together. We were twenty-one and twenty but didn't feel it.

The blessing was that we were together, and we were on our way home.

It seems like so long ago now.

The beautiful thing about mine and Adrian's life together then was that for the next few years, it was just us.

We needed that.

I couldn't recount all the adventures we went on as a couple, because there were so many. Adrian has always been a planner, and I believe now that all those hiking expeditions, visits to Disneyland and road trips were his way, as a very young man, of keeping us busy and moving us forward. He was taking care of the situation, like any loving hero would do.

One day while Adrian was doing PT with his unit, his heart rate skyrocketed to the point that emergency medication to slow it didn't work. The scare sent us to heart specialists, and it was determined my dearest needed a procedure to fix the electrical node controlling his heart rate.

Simply put, it was so strange—to think that this was our reality. But, we pushed along and hoped for the best, looking forward to the ablation procedure. Adrian was my rock. He couldn't have a broken heart. It would be fixed.

Ever since we'd married, we'd been stationed far away from family, even when we returned stateside. So it was always just the two of us. And I'd been leaning on him for so long. But no questions asked, if it was now going to be my turn to be the rock, I would dive headfirst into that role.

Two weeks before Adrian would turn twenty-six years old, the ablation was not successful and, instead of fixing the problem, made it worse. My soldier walked away from the hospital with a permanent pacemaker implanted in his chest and a heart that is completely dependent on that lifesaving battery.

The blessing was that he walked out of the hospital, and we were together.

I'll never forget the thoughtful doctor who came out and asked me what side Adrian held his rifle on so that he could implant the pacemaker on the opposite side. It was that action that allowed Adrian to fight to stay in the Army he loved and prove he could still perform his duties.

He was very lucky but also very lost. And now it was my turn not only to be supportive, but to anticipate his feelings and mood each day when he would come home.

I keep repeating that the blessing was we were together.

Some people say it's hard to believe how survivors get through the challenges they are faced with. But what I can't imagine is having to do it alone, and my heart goes out to anyone in that situation. Please know that if nothing else, you are in my family's thoughts and prayers.

Life soon found its balance again for us.

The Army allowed Adrian to change his job to a less-physical one, which in turn kept him from being medically discharged. And then in 2001, we were blessed with a full-term pregnancy. Because this time around we knew I had an incompetent cervix (when the weight of the growing baby becomes too heavy for the weak cervix to hold it inside the womb, it essentially falls out), Adrian sent me to live with my dad and stepmom in Oklahoma while he stayed stationed in Colorado. He didn't have to explain with words or admit out loud the reason. I understood Adrian was terrified of the past repeating itself and wanted me somewhere I could stay off my feet and have the constant attention of family. That was something Adrian couldn't provide as an active-duty soldier on call. I missed him, and it was upsetting at times, but my dad and stepmom were our guardian angels.

The blessing was threefold. I learned the value of accepting help when you so obviously need it. Our son was born healthy and on time, and I got to spend precious time with my dad.

As soon as he was old enough, we began adventures with our little one in tow. Disneyland wasn't just fun now, it was magical. We happily exchanged Guns N' Roses concerts for the Wiggles, nights of sleep for power naps, and Colorado/Oklahoma for Georgia. It was time to once again leave the western half of the U.S. and make it on our own. Our newly grown family was ready for a new place.

Life was balanced, which for the record is the way we prefer it. (Smile)

For all the ups and downs, we were always blessed with healthy-sized chunks of time together in between. If circumstances arose (like Adrian deploying to the invasion of Iraq) when we needed to love from afar, it wasn't long before togetherness followed.

That's not to say I didn't have times when I counted the good moments but wondered if heartbreak was waiting around the corner. I just tried to keep those to a minimum.

Luckily by this time, Adrian and I had learned that a balanced life required the good and the bad. And that we had always gotten though the rough patches hand in hand.

In 2007, that wouldn't be the case.

Adrian deployed for another year in Iraq, but not before depositing our son and me somewhere safe. This time it was back home in San Diego with Mom. I sometimes wonder if he had one of those feelings of what was to come.

A few months into that deployment, my dad was killed by a careless driver, one mile from his Oklahoma home, while riding his motorcycle. Adrian couldn't come home.

A few months after losing my dad, my paternal grandpa took his own life. Adrian still couldn't come home.

It sounds like a lot of couldn'ts, but I know now the blessing was learning love and support sometimes exist in simply knowing you are looking at the same glow of the same moon as your faraway hero.

For the remainder of that deployment, I told myself, "When he comes home, we'll deal with it then—when he comes home." I was lost, and this time, my dear mom was our guardian angel.

This year, my husband retired from the Army after twenty-one years of service.

The blessing is that he's a full-time online student now, earning his master's degree in counseling…and he's home all the time! That means he sees firsthand the creation of the romance heroes who always contain little bits of him.

I can't imagine my hero ever going away again. But if he does, it will be okay, because we've become old pros at sharing, loving from afar and accepting help. But, more important, we know how precious it is when you come home.

Blessings to you and yours from the Flores Family.

Carlene Love Flores is a fan of the stars (especially Orion), music (especially Depeche Mode), and her traveling family (no favorites—she loves them all). These inspire her intimate romance stories. If she could touch someone's heart with writing the way others have for her, she'd say there never lived a luckier girl.

Visit Carlene online at www.carlenelove.com.

Love Is All Around

Donna Grant

One of my favorite lines is from the movie *Love Actually*: "Love is all around."

I grew up with loving parents, who after fifty-four years of marriage are still together. They gave me the foundation for a steady marriage and helped me see what I wanted in a husband/marriage. Of course, knowing it and finding it are two different things.

Who knew in June of 1995, as I sat in a special summer session in college, that my life would change in the blink of an eye? For me, it was another day, and hopefully a quick few weeks on a course I had been putting off. I was thinking of the weekend and my plans with friends. But everything stopped the moment I laid eyes on a hunky guy with the brightest blue eyes I had ever seen.

As soon as Steve walked into that class, I knew one definitive thing: I was going to marry him. I used to hear people say that all the time, and I'd just roll my eyes, thinking, "As if!" The truth is that it happened to me. It wasn't a lightning bolt, earthquake, or anything so extreme. It was simply warmth that spread through me as if recognizing the other half of myself, a half I hadn't even realized was missing until that moment.

When he turned those blue eyes on me and smiled, I was prepared to do whatever it took to get his attention. Luckily, he felt the same, and it wasn't long before we were dating, engaged, and then married. Like so many in the military, Steve was divorced with a young daughter. After serving our country for six years in the Marine Corps, he had returned home to rebuild his life. We both knew the road would be difficult, but we forged ahead, shoulder to shoulder, side by side.

There were too many bumps to count, some huge potholes, a few dips, but always we had each other. There was a lot of laughter and love. Steve has a wicked sense of humor that always has me laughing. It was that laughter that forged our bond tighter as we had children of our own.

There are times I look at Steve and think we've only been together a short time, that we're still newly married. Then I look at our oldest, now fourteen, and realize that we just celebrated seventeen years of marriage. Other times, I feel as if he's always been in my life, that I've known him forever. That there was never a day he wasn't beside me.

I think it's the little things we do for each other that keep things romantic, sexy, and intriguing. We still hold hands everywhere we go, even in the car. He opens doors for me, cooks, and often surprises me with flowers at the oddest times. We talk several times during the day on the phone while he's at work. Mostly, it's to check in and see how each other's days are going.

We have frequent date nights that can include dinner, a movie, a long drive, or even staying at home, if the kids are gone, and snacking on bread and cheeses with a glass of wine and a great movie.

There are times we'll be at a party and separated, and yet I'll look over to find him smiling at me before he mouths, "I love you." It's a "just us" moment in a crowd of people, a spark that continues to sizzle years after our first kiss.

When we recognized that the dining room in our house wasn't being used but once a year, we converted it into our Wine Room. Now filled with chairs, sofas, a wall full of pictures of our family during each of our vacations, and stocked with wine, it has become one of our favorite rooms.

Each night before dinner, Steve and I head into that room for a glass of wine and to talk about our day, the kids, what we have going on the next day, and any plans we're making. It doesn't take long before the kids are in there with us, sharing their day and the happenings at school.

A room that was normally forgotten has turned into a thriving heart of our home, a place where there's no TV. There's just lots of talking.

It's that communicating that is the cornerstone of our relationship. We tell each other everything, no matter how hard it is to hear or say. It's so easy to get upset and let things fester until it can destroy a relationship. It's a rule we put into place while we were still dating that we would share everything.

I knew it was important, but I didn't realize how vital such a rule was until years later. There are no secrets between us. He might get angry at something I did or said, but he will tell me and we'll work it out. The same goes for me. It has prevented us from fighting. We bicker, because, well, people bicker. That's normal. But the screaming, shouting kind of fights? Not a one. When there is open communication, so much gets resolved before it can grow into something ugly and destructive. And we never, ever go to bed angry at each other.

It was Steve who urged me to write my first story. His support has never waivered. He reads my books and also helps me work out scenes when I'm stuck. He's my go-to guy when I'm writing a fight scene.

We celebrate every book release, every contract, and every good thing that happens in my career. And, in turn, we do the same for him in his career and the triathlons in which he competes. We're each other's best friend, and while we each have our own group of friends, we rarely do something without the other.

There's another rule we have in our marriage: no electronics in the bedroom. That means even a TV. Our bedroom is our sanctuary. It's a place the kids know is ours, a place where we can get away when needed.

Our bedroom is where the outside world, with all the gadgets, phones, e-mail, and intrusions, doesn't penetrate. I believe this is one of the biggest reasons we still have such a loving marriage. We're both on our computers all day long, and it would be so easy to bring the laptop or iPad in the bed and get some more work done, but we don't. Everyone needs time to disconnect from life and reconnect with each other, and every night we get ours.

Love isn't all about sex. Love is about knowing someone as well as you know yourself, being there for them in the good times and the bad, caring for them when they're healthy as well as when they are ill.

It's about realizing life isn't just about you anymore.

It's about the *both* of you.

I've been asked so many times if my marriage factors into the heroes I write. The answer is yes! I love men who take charge, men who will stop at nothing to care for the ones they love—the alphas. I married such a man, and it's no wonder that all of my heroes are alphas. However, just like my heroes, Steve is loving, considerate, affectionate, devoted, funny, charming, successful, and sexy as hell.

I still get all tingly when he kisses me. I still long to hold his hand. I still gaze into his dazzling blue eyes. I still curl up next to him on the couch. I still cuddle in bed. I still look for things to give him that will make him smile. I still kiss him every time he leaves and when he comes home. I still say, "I love you," when getting off the phone.

I still get excited when he walks through the door, shouting, "Baby, I'm home!"

Three simple rules have helped shape my marriage into what it is today:

1. Open communication.
2. Never go to bed angry at each other.
3. No electronics in the bedroom.

Life isn't always simple, but facing the challenges with someone who is the other part of your soul makes it a lot less frightening and easier to face. Just knowing we have each other, that we support each other in whatever decisions are made, that we face nothing alone, brings us together every day.

Love *is* all around us. We just have to know how to see it, how to feel it, how to return it, and, most important, how to share it.

New York Times and *USA Today* bestselling author Donna Grant has been praised for her "totally addictive" and "unique and sensual" stories. She's the author of more than twenty-five novels spanning multiple genres of romance. Her bestselling series, *Dark Kings*, features a thrilling combination of shape-shifting, immortal dragons who are dark, dangerous, and irresistible. She lives with her husband, two children, a dog, and three cats in Texas.

Visit Donna at www.donnagrant.com.

Working Our Way to a Happily Ever After

Cindy Nord

She went back in time to find him.

At thirty years old, betrayed and disillusioned by real-life romance, a history-loving divorcée, mother of two rambunctious young sons, and an avid reader of love stories, immersed herself in writing a Civil War novel that contained all the elements she believed a true hero should possess. Each night she would tuck the boys into bed, then pull out her typewriter and add a few more lines to a story carved deep inside her heart.

Then one day, a miracle happened, though at the time she didn't recognize it as such. News reached her of a Civil War reenactment taking place on the grounds of the local university. She could hardly believe her luck. *This* was a perfect opportunity to learn firsthand about the tumultuous time period that held her interest. So...clutching hold of her boys' hands, she headed straight for the event.

Excitement pulsed in her veins as American history breathed into life. The acrid aroma of campfires wafted around her. The thundering gallop of cavalry horses and the blazing retort of musketry echoed in her ears. Women clad in breathtaking Victorian gowns sashayed across the grounds and stole the show.

Indeed, a fascinating spectacle swept her straight back into the nineteenth century.

And then, a spark ignited when she saw a handsome Federal officer marching across the field, leading his soldiers into battle. At that moment, she knew she would become part of this most unique hobby. She and the boys immediately *joined up*, and a remarkable friendship with the handsome officer soon developed.

Their first telephone conversation lasted more than an hour; each conversation thereafter, longer still. Although reluctant to jump into any kind of relationship again, she nonetheless found their incredible friendship blossoming into so much more.

A few months later, her two boys walked her down the aisle and into the waiting arms of her real-life hero.

This was how the love story between Tom and Cindy Nord began.

Ambling into a ready-made family was not the easiest thing for a single guy to do, but Tom came in with eyes and arms wide open. Twenty-plus years later, the boys are grown and on their own, we're blessed with three amazing grandchildren, and the promises we made to one another so long ago are still an integral part of our lives.

So, how *did* we make our marriage flourish, when many others around us have failed? Well, here are a few of the things that we believe have helped to keep us close.

First and foremost, my husband is my best friend. And I know, without a shadow of a doubt, that I am his. This truth has never waned in all these years. Somewhere along the way, we discovered we had turned into a phenomenal mutual-support team. That partnership became the glue that sealed us through all the years of teenage angst, broken-down cars, and broken parental rules.

As a writer, I am a passionate soul. And Tom? Well, Tom is the calm that tempers my storm. This balancing act has worked well with all that life has thrown at us. Where he is my anchor, I am his sail, pushing him, helping him, encouraging him to forge in new directions.

Second, we make each other laugh. Whether it be a silly song we both start singing at the exact same time or a corny joke only we find funny, these are the golden threads sewing us together. Strong. Solid. Unbreakable. We have come to cherish every single strand.

But, okay...I know what you're thinking. Do we ever fight? Of course we fight. And we fight loud and hard, too, fervent about whatever point we are trying to make at that moment. Yet, as the years rolled along, we came to understand that disagreements, however unpleasant at the time, didn't mean *the end*. Forgiveness always followed as we learned how to communicate.

Yep. Number three: communication, which reminds me of a funny story. Tom and I had been married only a couple of years when someone at work mentioned an upcoming marriage-enrichment encounter offered at a noted retreat center. The event included lessons to help couples communicate better. *What a great idea!* Straightaway, we signed up.

The time arrived. We drove fifty miles to the campus. With high expectations about what we might learn to deepen our relationship, we clutched hands and headed into our first workshop. After sitting through eight grueling hours listening to instructors telling couples how to talk to one another, we returned to our dorm room realizing we didn't really have a problem in that department after all, unlike some of the others in attendance. Rather than face another lengthy session or waste any more of our precious time, that evening we plotted our escape.

The next morning after breakfast, we gave our well-rehearsed excuses and stole away. And the remainder of the weekend found us *beautifully communicating* at a nearby resort and spa.

The point of all this is that we had already learned, early on, how to pry open the other to allow our needs and desires to flow out. If anything, the retreat simply solidified this fact.

Many years later, we still get a chuckle when thinking about that illuminating weekend adventure.

That brings me to number four on our countdown list of how we make things work. Mutual interests. Obviously, the love of history is one of them. Since we met on a mock *battlefield*, Civil War reenacting dominated our early years. As time went on, however, we moved away from dressing up and living the history into a more relaxed routine that didn't involve wearing corsets or marching in the blazing sun.

As a couple, we were evolving. Our interests had room to expand. *Wow. This was going to be fun!* We found time to visit museums and other cultural sites together. When the kids went to bed, we shared reading and research ideas over glasses of wine. Tom's interest in all things militaria advanced. He became an avid collector of artifacts. I bought him a metal detector. Off he went, digging up Civil War belt buckles and cannonballs, ancient coins and other buried treasures. His amazing collection grew.

During this time, my interest in Victorian fashions and the role of women in society deepened. I became a lecturer, sharing my knowledge of the things I learned along the way. Tom supported me wholeheartedly in my endeavor. Our analogous passions once again fused us as our appreciation of those bygone eras played an important role in our future. To this day, we still can't pass a historical marker without stopping to *peek into the past*.

And then there are our traveling adventures. Ah yes… another wonderful interest that blossomed for us over the years. We took the kids to amusement parks, enjoyed romantic Caribbean cruises, and even roamed across America in a recreational vehicle we fondly call Bodie. These, along with a love of nature and gardening, have helped to strengthen our bond even more.

And now I've reached number five: keeping active. Indeed, another key in our relationship arsenal. From walking with our Shelties, to picking out smoothie recipes including vegetables Tom had rarely heard of before (kale, anyone?), to researching a nutraceutical supplementation program that seems to ward off colds and other diseases, I've enjoyed coming up with ideas and activities to keep us healthy. Over the years, our varied adventures have kept us vibrant. We've enjoyed bicycling, scuba diving, canoeing, hiking, and zip-lining through the treetops at warp speed. We've documented these pastimes with enough photos to fill the Grand Canyon. We even tried white-water rafting. Once. Although Tom thoroughly enjoyed his invigorating journey down the rapids in the eight-man inflatable raft, the trip video we purchased at the gift shop following our escapade clearly revealed a different reaction from me. I was the only passenger in obvious, abject terror, clutching the side of the yellow raft as I screamed my way down the churning length of the Gauley River. Needless to say, white-water rafting is no longer on the list of things Tom and I will be enjoying together anytime soon. In this case, individuality inside a relationship is also a very good thing.

Now, remember that Civil War novel I mentioned I was writing at the beginning of this article? Well, I finished it, then promptly put it in a box and shoved it under my bed, where it remained for several years. Until one evening, at the encouragement of my husband, I reached under the mattress, pulled the manuscript out and blew off the dust. *No Greater Glory*. I'd always liked the title; it seemed a true reflection of my life with Tom. After a little touching up, and with a kiss and a prayer, I mailed the complete story to the Romance Writers of America's national Golden Heart contest. Six months later, I received a call telling me my love story was one of nine historical finalists. *Oh my gosh…somebody better pinch me.*

Another chapter in our lives was about to be written.

From this contest I secured a New York agent, who quickly sold my manuscript to a publishing house. Now, I was a bona fide author.

Book signings, social media and personal appearances soon followed.

Since my first novel is a Civil War romance, some of the invitations came from museums, antebellum homes, and universities. Because of his expertise in that time period, I asked Tom to come along with me. He agreed. Together, we planned out an intriguing way for him to participate.

He opened the program with a show-and-tell of the muskets, swords, cannonballs, and other artifacts he'd brought with him from his extensive collection. After his demonstration, I finished up by discussing Victorian fashions and gave a reading from my book. Both entertaining and educational, the tie-in worked perfectly.

Our little "dog and pony" show was born.

Since then, we've become a seasoned presentation team, bringing greater depth to my book-reading and signing events. Our program even has expanded from the local level to national venues.

It seems I've come full circle: from having a dream about writing the perfect hero to actually sharing my everyday life with one. Together, Tom and I are making this marriage work. He supports me in all my writing endeavors, and I am blessed to have his incredible strength and love.

No one's marriage is perfect. Ours certainly isn't. We both have our faults, but learning how to overlook some and having the willingness to change others is extremely important.

Our connection is an ongoing work in progress. Just like writing a book. Possessing a caring and open heart is what Tom and I have found helps to keep our relationship humming along.

We try to do the best we can.

In the end, that's all anyone can do.

Cindy Nord's bestselling debut novel, *No Greater Glory*, was featured on *USA Today*'s Happily Ever After romance fiction blog and for nearly a year was the #1 Civil War Romance at Amazon. A luscious blend of history and romance, her stories meld both genres around fast-paced action and emotionally driven characters. Yes, true love awaits you in the writings of Cindy Nord.

Visit Cindy online at www.cindynord.com.

Resting Easy

K.M. Jackson

Coming to bed at the end of the day after a long hot soak to wash the fatigue off and ease aged joints, I step into the bedroom, wondering out loud to my husband, "Where did the past week go? How did it get by us so fast?" I don't get a reply. I glance at my husband as he lies in our bed. His lashes fan out, resting on smooth cheeks. His lips are relaxed in contentment, and I glance down to see his chest rising and falling in an easy, rhythmic motion. Despite a small twinge of annoyance over the fact that he didn't wait up for me, I can't help but smile to myself. Here, now, relaxed and quiet as he is, he looks soothed and at peace and every bit the young man I met over twenty years ago. No trace of the stressed-out man who was sifting through the bills an hour before. Looking at him now, my heart takes on a soothing sway.

Then my eyes shift as I look down at his hand clutched tightly around the television remote, and a frown twists at the corner of my lips. Glancing up at the TV, I see he's once again fallen asleep midturn, and the TV is paused on a station where neither of us understands the language. I shake my head. It's so him. He goes and goes all day until he can't take one more step, only to fall dead asleep, wake up and do it all over again the next day. I wonder how long he can run himself ragged.

Carefully, I get into bed and try to ease the remote from his hand, only to have his eyes pop open, latching on to mine as his grip tightens possessively. "I was watching that."

I shake my head. "No, it was watching you. Care to give me a recap to prove it?"

He groans as his eyes soften, and he loosens his grip, knowing I've won this one. "No, sorry, it's just I'm so tired, and I have to get up and do it again tomorrow."

I lean over and kiss him gently as I ease away the remote. "I know, and for this I'm grateful."

"Yeah, me, too."

The TV is turned off, and as one we turn together. One spooned in the other's embrace. Knowing within a few hours the spoon will be flipped, and it will be other way around. He spoons me, I spoon him. It's a dance we do in our sleep to let each other know the other is still there. That it doesn't matter who's behind or who is in front. All that matters is that one is there for the other. With love, support and protection while we are at our most vulnerable, in sleep.

Statistics tell us nowadays that people are marrying less, later and divorcing more. These days the idea of marriage feels at times temporary, just a thing for the season and then on to the next when that trend wears out. Now of course I know people go into marriage with plans of forever, but in the back of their minds and in the minds of others, there is always a contingency plan, and please don't get this jaded romantic wrong, having a plan B is fantastic and we often need a plan C and D. But how often do we hear, "Is this the first, second or third marriage?" for John or Jane as they head down the aisle, eyes brimming with hope again?

So with short-term marriages being more the norm, my husband and I going on to the twenty-fifth-year mark (ack, a quarter of a century) have turned into quite the oddity, a fun couple to have at dinner gathering to stare at and ask questions of as if we are relics unearthed from days gone by. As if we're some sort of fifties flashback one should sit at the knee of and marvel over and hang on their every word as we dole out the magic formula to racking up the years. (Trust me, there are times when we marvel ourselves.)

The main question we get is: How have we made it last for as long as we have, getting over the honeymoon stage and the seven-year itch and the eleven-year boredom stretch that usually take down even the most golden of marriages? Often, I joke and laugh this question off. Saying cutesy little things like, "Oh, he's just an old habit by now" or "I always told him if we divorce, he gets the kids." Lines that make people chuckle and move on. But, really, there are no quick quips to sum up how you go from year one to year twenty-five. It's just life and life done diligently. Like a habit, or like our nightly remote-control tug-of-war, being in any long-term relationship takes humor, patience, understanding, some serious work and even more serious play.

When I met my husband, I was young and not-so-bright-eyed, and I will admit to not being the marriage-age statistic of twenty-seven that is out today. Slightly less jaded than I am now but still with plenty of sass, I was pushed out into the job market, ironically, by my favorite high school literature teacher, the late Frank McCourt. One day he caught me sulking in the hall and asked what was wrong. When I went on about my lack of funds and general malaise about life, he directed me to the school job board and pointed out a part-time law firm accounting job that he assured me I was smart enough to handle. With his advice to buck up, I was sent on my way Uptown to Park Avenue and my future in the guise of a charming, shy, Southern IT manager.

At the firm I stuck out like a sore thumb with my dyed, spiky hair, homage-to-Prince blouses, and tight, ripped jeans. But still, there in that unlikely place, I met someone (my future husband) who would turn out to be both my polar opposite, in his pinpoint button-downs and pleated khakis, and my mirror image. It is said in Corinthians 13 that love is patient and kind, that it always protects, trusts, hopes and perseveres. This has truly been a way, both consciously and unconsciously, my husband and I have approached our relationship and our marriage.

You start out as friends, bright and sunny and both loving the same movies or putting on a good face to pretend to love the same movies. But what happens when the bright and sunny starts to fade into the everyday routine cycle of work, eat, sleep? This is when things get tricky and the mind gets antsy. You look around and wonder, where did my friend go? That is when I believe the patience and the kindness come into play, and you have to let the annoyance go and look at life through the eyes of your partner. You see where the other could be overworked and, instead of chiding, you slip that remote away and spoon your love with kindness and understanding.

Now what about when life brings you unexpected surprises as it did for us twenty years ago, when pregnant and having my first sonogram, I was asked by my technician, "How many children do you want to have?" Now there's an odd one to get while you're nervous and cold with a belly covered in jelly. My answer was, "One, of course," but who knew that it was Baby BOGO Day, and the hubs and I were indeed pregnant with twins? This was a moment when it was time to fall on trust. Trust in each other and in what the Universe had in store for our rapidly growing family. It was hold-on-tight time and don't let go.

It was just days after bringing our twins home and the hubbub had died down and we were now left alone, and I'll admit a little nervous, with our two beautiful babies. We had set up two wicker bassinets in our bedroom to make it easier to get the babies when feeding time came, and believe me, with twins, it was always feeding time. After yet another round with my son, it was the middle of the night and I was practically passed out, dead asleep.

But I awoke to the sound of my daughter crying, her wailing permeating my subconscious. Groggy, I was about to get up from the bed to go and get her when I blinked and noticed that my husband was already there. He was down on his knees on the floor, gently rocking her bassinette back and forth as he pleaded with her to please go back to sleep. I could hear the desperation and the exhaustion in his voice, and it made me humble to see this big, proud man on his knees in a position of surrender to this tiny human. Inwardly, I laughed at the odd sight before me, though at the same time, my heart opened up just a little wider knowing how much of himself he would sacrifice for us. I then asked if he needed me to get up and help, but he softly said no, that he knew I was tired and needed rest and he would care for us. I nodded and went back to sleep. I don't know when my daughter stopped crying, but that night I slept like a baby, trusting that he had us. That he was there watching over us and could be for years to come. No matter what.

Then you have the times when life throws you other curves, such as financial hardships or the tragedy of a loved one being ill. Here is a time when protection and hope have to take action. Hope that, with each other, hard work and holding on tight, you will make it to another day and a brighter one. And you both will, but it takes perseverance. You see, I was only half-joking when I said we were an old habit, or if we were to get divorced he'd get the kids. Now, he knows I'd never give up my children, but this was my way of reminding him and the world that parenting is a team effort, just like our marriage is, and we are in it together. Many of my most vivid memories with my husband come from moments over the years when I have been either mentally or emotionally exhausted, and he's been there to give me the oxygen that I needed. Always my knight in shining and, at times, tarnished armor, but still my knight. That beacon in the darkness and the hand I have to hold. My teammate and my helpmate. The one who let me rest those years ago when I so desperately needed it, and the one I pry the remote from now.

And here we are once again, another late night. Back in the bedroom, there are no more bassinettes, no more wailing babies, just a blaring television, an exhausted man and a patient wife telling him to turn over.

Go back to sleep. I'll take care of you tonight.

K.M. Jackson

A native New Yorker, K.M. spent her formative years on the A train going from her home in Washington Heights to The Village where she attended Stuyvesant High School. On that long ride to study math and science, K.M. had two dreams: to be a fashion designer and to be a writer. K.M. went on to study fashion design at FIT and spent ten years designing for various fashion houses. After having twins, K.M. took the leap of faith and decided to pursue her other dream of being a writer. She currently lives in a suburb of New York with her husband, twins, and a precocious terrier named Jack that keeps her on her toes.

When not writing, she can be found on Twitter @kwanawrites and on her website at www.kwana.com.

For Better or For Worse

Heather McCollum

We met in college after I'd experienced way too much heartache as a teen drawn to all the bad boys. Braden is one of the good guys, so it took a year of his friendship before I woke up and saw the sexy hero walking next to me across the quad. But I finally did, and we kissed, and four years later I walked in white brocade down a candlelit aisle toward him. Our families stood on their respective sides. Only his mother was absent, for she'd died of breast cancer when he was nine years old.

When I was asked, "For better or for worse," and I answered with a heartfelt, "I do," I smiled at my squeaky-new husband, feeling fluttery and thrilled to be starting an adventure with my official partner in life. I was definitely living in the "better" season as I stared happily into my real Highland hero's chocolate-brown eyes.

Fast-forwarding through infertility, difficult pregnancies, and three babies later, we had built a solid life together. Work stress, squabbles about dishes and dirty underwear left on the floor kept the relationship real but still good. I released my first two romance novels and, despite turning forty, felt strong, sexy and confident. As a ridiculously busy couple, it was difficult to connect, so we joined an adult soccer team together. It was fun, time spent with my guy and five hundred and fifty calories burned at each game and practice. I loved it.

I exercised every day and finally slimmed down to the lowest jean size I'd ever fit in. I knew that on certain, non-bloated times of the month, I could tug on those skinny jeans with relative ease. So when that time came, and I had to suck in to close the button, I pouted and swore to add sit-ups to my routine. Turning forty did not mean I had to gain forty.

I ran with my bouncy rescue dog, worked in sit-ups and played soccer with Braden. It took a week before I noticed the pain on my right side, an ovulation-type pain that pinched more when I sat down than when I stood. So I just stood more. Who had time to sit with three kids anyway?

"Something doesn't feel right down here," I told my friend as I ran a hand over my abdomen. "I think I'm getting a bladder infection."

"Go to the doctor."

"When I have time," I answered, knowing that I never had time.

During the soccer playoffs, a big guy, nearly as tall and broad as Braden, kicked the ball toward my face. I managed to deflect it with my hand, and we thought I'd broken my wrist. I had no choice. I had to go to the doctor.

I sat on the crinkly, papered exam table while the nurse practitioner gently moved my sore wrist. "I don't think it's broken, but we should get an X-ray to rule out a fracture."

"Oh, and while I'm here," I said while she probed with cool fingers. "I think I'm getting a bladder infection. I've been bloated, and I have this twinge of pain on my right side."

"Let's take a feel. Lie back." And her cool fingers moved to my abdomen. "Hmm…" she said, her smile fading. "Something doesn't feel right."

My life became a windup toy, wound to the limit and then set down to whirl on a flat surface. An ultrasound the next morning found a five-inch mass on my ovary. *Five inches!* Five inches that hadn't been there less than six months before at my GYN visit.

Braden drove me immediately to my GYN. "It looks complex," the doctor said as he examined my films. "I want you to see a GYN oncology surgeon tomorrow." *Oncologist?!*

Braden drove me home. After I gave a quick, teary update to my mom, she continued to watch the kids while Braden and I retreated to sit on the steps of our back deck. It was late March, the world fresh and green. Birds chirped in our Leland pines and swooped down from the tall oak by the play set. My herbs waved in the light breeze, and daffodils bloomed along the fence. We sat there, next to each other on the steps, in silence. His hand found mine, warm and solid, as we stared outward at the world together. How different it suddenly looked.

"I'm scared," I whispered.

"So am I," he answered.

We met the oncologist the next morning. Since I was relatively young and healthy, she helped me hope for the best but also had the expertise to handle the worst. I would have the mass, which I'd named "Chucky," removed in a week. I was sent home to take it easy so as not to rupture Chucky inside me. *Okay?!*

Monday morning I drove to a bookstore to write, trying to continue on as if I wasn't carrying around a grapefruit-size time bomb in my abdomen. I drank a large chai latte, my favorite comfort drink, and proceeded to not write much of anything. Soon, my bladder began to fill. I called Braden fifteen minutes later after a trip to the bathroom.

"I can't pee," I whispered into my cell phone.

"What?"

"I can't pee. I just drank a huge latte and have to go, but I can't." Panic had crept into my voice, making it crack.

"Can you drive?"

"I think so."

"Drive to the doctor. I'll meet you there if you still can't go."

An hour later, I was nearly speechless, except for whimpers, as he drove me to an emergency room. They drained almost two liters of urine from my spasm-racked bladder. For two hours, Braden enticed me to drink foul-tasting contrast juice for a CT scan while I floated on a lovely drug, of which they wouldn't tell me the name for fear I'd be tempted to find it outside a hospital room. When it was time to go home with a catheter bag strapped to my leg, I couldn't walk nor could Braden cram me back into my jeans.

"Take the blanket," the nurse said, and Braden wrapped me like a burrito in a rough hospital blanket. They wheeled me out in a wheelchair, and he drove me home. I don't remember the drive. I do remember not being able to exit his truck. With my neighbors, mother, and kids flustered in the driveway, Braden lifted me, hero-style, and carried me up all fifteen steps to my bed.

A week later I had my surgery. Chucky had to go! "The surgery should take an hour and a half, unless we find that it is more than a benign mass," the surgeon told us. I watched her face for signs of concern, but she'd played this game before and gave nothing away. "If it is cancer, I will send a nurse out to tell you, Mr. McCollum, that everything is going well but it will be longer."

They hooked me up to tubes, me tearing up while Braden cracked jokes to ease the tension, since I was crazy-scared of needles. I floated off to a blissful sleep. Braden had the hard part. He had to stay awake. He had to be the one who nodded and listened while the nurse told him that everything was going well, but the surgery would take longer than anticipated. The hour and a half turned into five hours. When I woke, racked with pain, in a room instead of the recovery area after surgery, I knew something was wrong. "I'm in a room. This isn't good," I murmured.

And then Braden shared the worst thing to ever hit us, the before-and-after moment that changed our lives forever. "It's ovarian cancer," he said, and squeezed my hand. I stared into his chocolate-brown eyes and felt the waves of pain and terror crash down on me.

All day, he lifted me out and set me back in the hospital bed each time I had to use the bathroom and the three times I had to walk so they'd let me go home. He asked the doctor questions when I was too scared to say more than, "I have a four-year-old. Please. I can't die." For days at home, the pain was so fierce that if I tensed up to cry, I couldn't breathe. Braden set a rule for any and all visitors: "You must smile. No crying or you can't see her. She can't breathe when she cries."

I enrolled in a clinical trial to up my odds of surviving, which included five months of weekly, six-hour chemo treatments and then ten more months of chemo treatments every three weeks. A second surgery placed a port-a-cath in my chest so the meds could be piped directly into my jugular, saving my veins. I started giving myself gold stars every time I was stuck to help me deal with my phobia of needles. It worked for potty training my three kids, so it could work for me. My glorious, long, curly hair began to fall out after the second treatment. Braden and our ten year-old son shaved their heads the same day Braden shaved mine. We celebrated the chemo working to kill cancer cells with a little party of friends in the backyard.

Braden, who had never even liked mowing the lawn, built me a garden around our patio and erected bird feeders where I could sit and watch. He guarded my exposure to negative statistics on ovarian cancer (almost everything about OC is gloom and doom). He fielded questions, kept track of details and encouraged me to blog, because he knew I was happier writing. I found I could write only about how I was going to survive. My fiction writing was put on hold.

And in the dark, at night, after the kids were asleep, when I'd fall apart crying and shaking, he'd pull me into his lap and slowly glue me back together with his words. "We got it in time. You have the best doctors. The chemo is working. You are stronger than the cancer. You are beautiful. I love you."

"I'm scared," I cried into his shirt as he gently stroked my sore, bald head through my fuzzy sleeping hat.

"It's terrifying being on this side of it," he answered. "I can't imagine how scary it must be on your side."

Honest. Real. Always positive. Every time I needed him to put me back together, he did. Every time I needed the words, he gave them, feeding them to me like strength pills to keep me walking through the fire I was enduring. I suffered ulcers through my digestive tract, non-healing cuts in my burning mouth, a six-month sore throat, dizziness, pain through my whole body, fingernails that turned brown and fell off, a forty-pound weight gain from the steroids, bloody noses, and fear that I would leave my three kids without a mom, just like Braden's mom had done unwillingly to him.

I've met numerous cancer warriors during my two years of treatment and recovery. Several women suffered further by losing their support in the face of such an ordeal, their husbands being too afraid to face cancer with their wives. Terrible memories of his mother's death at such a young age could have swamped Braden, but instead he chose to do what he couldn't as a nine year-old child. He chose to fight—hard, maybe as hard as I was. I realized this as I sat in my garden, watching the birds I'd come to know so well, blogging about how I was fighting to live. And my love for Braden grew.

"For better or for worse." It is an oath that is rarely thought about during the sparkly happiness of youthful love, when feelings are new and couples spend a lot of time gazing into each other's eyes.

"For better or for worse." It is an oath that must be clung to when the giant wave is bearing down. When you can't tear your eyes away from catastrophic fear and you reach next to you and take hold of that hand that grasps for your own. That is love.

Love, real connection with another soul, does not mean gazing at one another, seeing only the beauty, enduring only the "better" seasons. Real love means looking out at life together, staring at the beautiful and the ugly through even the "worse" seasons and continuing to hold each other's outstretched hands.

I am thankfully in remission from my cancer. My constant pain has ebbed, and I have regained most of my hair and strength. I lost internal organs along the way but have gained a deeper understanding of what living joyfully really means. I came through the fire with scars but have grown more beautiful in my spirit. I thought when I married Braden nearly two decades ago that I loved him with all my heart, but I've realized, after holding his hand through these last two years, that I love him a thousand times more.

Heather McCollum is an award-winning, historical paranormal romance writer. She is a member of Romance Writers of America and was a 2009 Golden Heart Finalist. When she is not creating vibrant characters and magical adventures on the page, she is roaring her own battle cry in the war against ovarian cancer. Heather recently slew the cancer beast and resides with her very own hero and their three kids in the wilds of suburbia on the Mid-Atlantic coast.

Visit her online at
www.heathermccollum.com.

Soul Mates for a Thousand Lifetimes
(or, Diary of Two Cosmic Stalkers)

Nikoo & Jim McGoldrick

The young woman walked along the storm-strewn beach, her chestnut hair lifting gently in the breeze. In the distance, she spotted an old wooden boat that had washed ashore in the storm. Someone was trying to maneuver the aging, salt-encrusted craft back into the water. As she drew closer, the mysterious figure stood and pushed his hair off of his face. A handsome young man returned her gaze.

This is how we first met.

Well, actually, this is the lie we've told dozens of times to numerous publications about how we first met.

During a cable interview, another lie surfaced. With a perfectly straight face, Jim told the interviewer that he went online thirty-five years ago to get a mail-order bride through Persian-Wife.com. There were no dot-coms thirty-five years ago, but that didn't stop him from telling this whopper, or from going on to say that "when Nikoo arrived, we still had to wait until she turned seven to marry."

Enough lies.

For the first time, we're putting the truth in print. The truth is…he and I are soul mates. And we don't mean this in some trendy, superficial, clichéd way. We're not like those twenty-first-century fledgling amorists who stumble serendipitously onto a one hundred and forty-character cyber message that is so imbued with profundity that instantaneous and endless love follows…until the "unfriending" comes. No. Ours are the souls that have been skimming through the universe for uncounted lifetimes, pinging off each other and returning to connect again and again.

And we have lots to report. Why else would we be writing romance in this lifetime?

To start with, neither of us believes there are any shortcuts or surefire, winning strategies for a great marriage. I can only share what we practice, what we preach, and what we believe has kept our relationship strong over decades…and all those cosmic lifetimes.

Long ago, Jim and I accepted that magic is not what happens in the first couple of years of marriage. That first stage is just one short hop along an unending journey. So, in no specific order of importance, here are some relevant points about this leg of our cosmic journey. In short, this is how we love.

I know…we both know…it's the two of us against the world.

Life happens. There's a Persian saying that goes, "If you think someone's life is perfect, it only means that you don't know them." We've been no exception to this rule. In the years that we've been together, our family has gone through an infant son's heart surgery, my cancer, and other tragedies that are too painful to speak of. Any one of these things can easily crumple individuals beneath their weight and tear a couple apart. Conscious commitment to each other is a basic ingredient lacking in many relationships. Unfortunately, it often remains unrecognized until the world falls off its axis.

In our case, we have been able to stand together. Each of us has acted as guardian angel for the other. In the midst of each trial, we remained focused on our love and communication, which was often difficult. Talking is hard when you *think* you're the only one feeling pain.

I remember when we were just married, we were driving along a country road in Stonington, Connecticut. The snow was an icy crust on the fields beyond the stone walls that lined the road. We were talking about how our marriage would be, and we decided right then that we would not allow walking away ever to be an option. And from the beginning, we *consciously* tried to give more to the other than we took. As the early years began to add up, we became stronger, feeling secure and protected, recognizing that our relationship was founded on a solid sense of unity. When we had to go into battle, we had the determination to fight and survive together.

We respect each other.

All relationships have their ups and downs, good and bad days, pleasures and frustrations. It's easy to be generous with our partner when life is going smoothly. And when we're upset, it's easy to lay blame on a partner, to abuse them emotionally and verbally. This extends to public ridicule, too—disrespecting each other, no matter how innocent or humorously intended. Among our family and friends, Jim is known as "perfect," and I am "flawless." Mission accomplished…even if the sound of gagging follows us around. We love it.

But that's not all of it. We're individuals. Some of us successfully achieve adulthood with relatively high self-esteem, while others do not. Some of us waltz through life with great, healthy egos, while some of us were apparently in the wrong line when that part of the psyche was being handed out. No matter. It's our job to be a bright mirror for our partner, reflecting all the beauty and talent that we see in them. Regardless of the difference in our level of education, or the fact that one of us is climbing high on the business ladder of success while the other is staying home, we need to hear our partner praise us, give us credit, appreciate us, love us, and voice it every day.

We make a daily habit of talking and listening to each other.

We each did our time working for big corporations. Team meetings, communication seminars, management training. We're believers in teamwork, be it building nuclear submarines, or teaching a large group of students, or raising our children, or working on our next novel. We've worked this team communication into our daily life. Cappuccino time, or tea time, or glass of wine time. Every day, three hundred and sixty-five days a year, we carve out at least fifteen minutes at the end of our workday to have "our" team meeting. We use this time to unwind, to tell each other about our day, about what lies ahead of us. Sometimes we even use this time to argue, ask questions, voice what has been bothering us. We're time travelers, not mind readers. It's unfair to have our partner guess why, all of a sudden, one of us is feeling insecure after a certain event or a certain comment struck us the wrong way. We try to listen. We ask questions to clarify things.

Going back to the "life happens" reference, carving out even fifteen minutes isn't always easy for families with two working parents and children running from one activity to the next. We've been there, done that. For us, those treasured minutes were found during dinnertimes, and during turning-off-the-television times. Yes, you read that correctly. Make no mistake, we love television. There is always something entertaining on. But there were several times when we canceled the cable. Granted, it was usually right after the baseball season ended (I hate to hear Jim cry), but we did it. Today, acting so rashly as to cut the cable could bring a visit from a state agency concerned about your children's welfare, but it has been known to happen. The precious minutes were there, we just had to dig for them.

It's okay to be passionate in a disagreement, but we never sleep on it.

Scenarios that include miffed, irked, hurt partners happen in every marriage. We have definitely had our moments. But we battle it out until it's over. We never sleep on an unsettled disagreement. Unresolved arguments grow roots and branches, and the fruit is poison.

We've accepted that a soul-mate relationship can be more intense than many relationships. Add to that the working relationship of writing together—living over the shop, we call it—and there can be fireworks. One of the fiercest battles we ever had in our marriage was over the location of a castle stairway in a story we were writing. In the midst of it, a reporter from *The New York Times* arrived to do a feature on us. "A conversation with the McGoldricks, in which sentences ricochet back and forth between the two, might be a metaphor for their writing process." Luckily, the woman didn't see the non-metaphorically sharp objects we'd put away a minute before she rang the doorbell. After she left, we went back at it…and somehow resolved it before bedtime.

The most important thing we've learned is that, even during highly emotional episodes, we can focus on resolving the problem. We can see beyond the bad moment. We refuse to hurt each other to win a point. And we don't allow troubles to fester and become *more* than what they are. Jim will tell you that this was a genetic triumph, as well as a personal victory. His Irish roots insist that he carry a grudge for five generations and across three continents, and continuing long after anyone remembers who slighted whom at some funeral in 1873.

We fall in love with each other's flaws.

I read this somewhere. No relationship is perfect, and here I have to refer to another one of my Persian grandmother's sayings. "He who wants a rose must respect the thorn."

The notion of changing our partner to what we want them to be has never worked for us. Change must come from within. Of course, we're both probably too stubborn to be changed by someone else, anyway. But, luckily, I love Jim exactly as he is, and he loves me the same way. We accept both the great and sometimes annoying qualities and tendencies we each have.

This doesn't mean that we don't complain about those things. It doesn't mean that we don't occasionally tease each other about them. We just would *never* complain publicly about the fact that I take my seat belt off as soon as we turn on to our street, which starts the car beeping immediately. Or that Jim has to check the traffic report on his iPhone before going to the convenience store a block from the house. Or that I love to spread my clothes on the chair, on top of the dressers, anywhere there is an available space. Or that Jim has everything in the house, from the closets (his closet) to the dishes, to the dog's toys, categorized by size, color, texture... And he's anal about it.

And the list goes on. But who wants to live with someone who is absolutely perfect, anyway? Or flawless?

We continue to build shared interests.

Responding to a question about how it was that we started writing together after being married thirteen years, Jim told a reporter, "All our married life we wanted to find something we could do together. So writing was a very natural evolution. I don't know why it took so long."

I know why...because before writing, there was rowing, quilting, baseball, Pac-Man, golf, chess, tennis, skiing, backgammon, restoring an old sailboat, and renovating houses. Since then, we've added yoga, furniture upholstering, Words with Friends, and a few other hobbies. Some of them stick, some of them don't. But that's okay. Finding things that we could do together has been our goal.

There's a dark side to this. Jim burned the chess game in the fireplace because I was winning too many games. After the third hole of golf, I choose to drive the cart only and take pictures, and I complain for the rest of the round that "I'm *really* hungry." I learned to row on the Charles River when I was four months pregnant with our firstborn because that was when (and apparently the only time) they were offering lessons. Jim's quilting stitches are much better than mine, but I won't admit it. We are both die-hard Red Sox fans (I joined the nation in 1985), and in 1986 we ate chicken on every game day (because Wade Boggs did) and spent our October mortgage payment buying playoff tickets. Incidentally, we're happy to say that this past decade has been much kinder to us (not in mortgage payments, but in being Sox fans).

We've come to the conclusion that as far as activities go, everything is better when we do it together.

We are *not* just friends.

We believe our friendship is the foundation of our marriage. But there's more. Physical contact, intimacy, passion are also key parts of it. It's important to cultivate romance. We've written thirty romance novels about it, so we won't explain it here.

Romance also means dating, but dating doesn't have to have a large price tag associated with it. An afternoon hike. An ice-cream cone. A drive to the beach. Okay, Jim might even think our weekly trip to Costco is romantic, but we also have our trips to the Caribbean. Next year, Europe. But whether it's a quiet dinner for two or a run to some fast-food place, we look for opportunities to spend time with each other.

We hug.

It's sort of fitting that we end this ramble with some praise for the unsung hero of affection. We believe in hugs. Long hugs. Every morning before the day starts…we hug. We read somewhere a long time ago that most couples cannot hug each other for more than a minute. We can. In holding on tight to each other, we acknowledge the essential presence of our partner and we close out the world.

It's just the two of us. Two cosmic travelers who have found their way home.

That's how we love.

Nikoo and Jim McGoldrick are storytellers, teachers, and partners in the truest sense. Together, they write historical romance as May McGoldrick and contemporary suspense thrillers as Jan Coffey. These prolific and popular authors have been the recipients of numerous awards for their work. They now reside in Litchfield County, Connecticut.

Visit their website at
www.nikooandjim.com.

Made in the USA
Las Vegas, NV
28 October 2024